"God does notice us, and He watches over us.
But it is usually through another that He meets our needs."

President Spencer W. Kimball

D0948092

This book is a transcript of a seminar given to the Arkansas Little Rock Mission in Little Rock. It is available free to missionaries through their mission presidents, or at cost to anyone else who would like it.

It is only available from:

Scott Marshall
2282 Whitten Rd.
Memphis, TN 38133
1-901-372-7421
Fax 901-372-6971
e-mail: MemphisBPC@AOL.com

This book is dedicated to my Savior Jesus Christ with thanks that he sent missionaries to find me.

TABLE OF CONTENTS

TABLE OF CONTENTS CONT.

CHAPTER ONE

WHO ARE YOU?

Brothers and Sisters: Do you know who you are? You are the finest people on the face of this planet. When you get up in the morning and look in the mirror, do you see yourselves as representatives of Jesus Christ?

Do you see yourselves as Bill, Tom, or Sue who used to live in Utah or Idaho or Montana, or do you see yourselves as a reflection of Jesus Christ?

(Holding up a picture of Jesus) This is who you are to people of the world. When they see you, they should see a reflection of the Savior. I can testify that I know that this is true, that you are representatives of Jesus Christ.

If we were to go out on the street and put up a roadblock, stop cars and pull the people out of them and say to them "We want you to stop what you are doing and go out and preach about Jesus Christ for two years. Plus, we are not going to pay you - in fact, you or your loved ones have to pay your way."

How many cars are we going to have to stop in order to find people willing to do that? 100? 200? 300? You are in the top one percent of all the people on the earth because you have an understanding of the purpose of life and who you are. You are literally children of our Father in Heaven. You love Him enough that you will come out and share that love with your brothers and sisters, even those who don't want to hear it.

1

When I went on my mission, my bishop had told me that I was too old (26) to go on a mission, the stake president had told me the same thing, so I found this lovely girl and was engaged to be married. I went to the bishop for a temple recommend to be married. The interview began and after a short while the bishop put down his pen and said, "You don't seem very excited about getting married."

I said, "Well, I am and she's a wonderful girl but I have realized that I won't be able to serve a full-time mission. I won't be able to give back as much as was given to me when the missionaries came to Indiana and taught me the Gospel. It so happened that he was a new bishop. My old bishop had been replaced. I also had a new stake president.

My bishop said "Just a minute," and picked up the phone. He called the new stake president and the next thing I knew - I was called on a mission. I went to see my fiancee and said: "Honey, I've got some good news and some bad news."

She asked, "What's the good news? I said, "The good news is that I passed the interview." Then she asked, "What's the bad news?" I said, "I'm going on a mission." She began to pound on my chest while saying she was too old to wait for a missionary. Well, that's another story.

I closed my Corvette business and went into the Mission Home where they pump you up. It was a wonderful, wonderful experience. They got us so enthused. They convinced us that we could baptize thousands.

When I arrived in the mission field, I got off the

plane and the mission president met me. I was the first missionary called to the new Missouri St. Louis Mission, that is, me and a missionary from Texas. President Olsen interviewed me and said, "Now, Elder Marshall, we would like for you to set a goal for baptisms while you are on your mission. How many baptisms would you like to have on your mission?"

I said, "President, I'm going to baptize thousands!" The mission up there is very much like here, (Arkansas). It's very difficult. The people have a lot of the same spirit. He didn't discourage me, instead, he put his arm around me, patted me on the back and said, "That's great, Elder Marshall, you go out there and get them!" He didn't tell me how hard it was going to be.

My first companion was Elder Mix, He was a great missionary. He had baptisms every month of his mission. He later became an assistant to the mission president.

We went to work and we worked real hard the first month. At the end of the month he shook his head and said, "I don't understand it, Elder. I have had baptisms every month of my mission until I got you. We need to work harder." So the next month we worked harder and at the end of the second month, he said, "Elder, I can't understand it. I baptized every month of my mission except the months since I met you."

I wondered "What am I doing wrong?" I got a new companion. This companion was great too. Later he also became an assistant to the President. We worked hard that third month and at the end, we hadn't had any baptisms. He said, "I can't understand it, Elder. I have had baptisms every month of my mission until I got you."

Three and a half months out, we had a Christmas Conference and the Mission President brought me in. I was really distressed and he could tell it. He said to me, "Elder Marshall, what's wrong? Why are you so down? Did you get a `Dear John' letter? I said, "No, President, worse than that. I've been out for three and a half months and I haven't had a baptism and I just don't know what to do."

He put his arm around me and pumped me up with his positive mental attitude and when I went out the door I was all excited again. I said, "President, I want you to know that even if I'm out for five months before I get a baptism, I'm still NOT going to get discouraged."

So I went out and the fourth month went by and no baptisms. The fifth month, and no baptisms. The sixth month and no baptisms. By that time I decided that if I had to go my whole mission and never have a baptism, at least I would be known as the most enthusiastic missionary they had ever seen in the mission, and that I would be able to go home knowing that I had given it all my heart, might, mind and strength. I had worked as hard as I possibly could. I would have no regrets and no excuses for not baptizing.

Seven months went by with no baptisms. At eight months out with no baptisms, I thought, "One-third of my mission is over and I haven't had a single baptism." I remembered painfully that I had told the President that I was going to baptize thousands. I thought, "What hope do I have now of ever setting a record in a mission field, except maybe the one for the longest time without a baptism."

Then a little over eight months out, I had my first baptism, and it wasn't from anything I did. It was virtually a self-referral. A girl came up to me in the grocery store on "P-Day" and asked us to come and teach her about the gospel. Of course, we about fell over. We assured her that we would. She was my first baptism!

My mission president always told us that we should follow up on our baptisms so they don't become inactive so I brought her with me today. I would like to promise you that she has not gone inactive and also I would like to emphasize that Sister Marshall and I kept all the mission rules concerning relationships with the opposite sex while I was on my mission. You will be blessed if you will "lock you hearts" while on your mission (see page 96).

What I hope you will gather from this is that no matter what discouragement you may have had at this point in your mission, it can change tomorrow. I believe that the Lord felt that I needed to be humbled. Perhaps He knew that some day I would be talking to you and He wanted to give me an experience that perhaps could relate to you. Whatever your circumstances are, they can change today, and you can have great success and great happiness in your missionary labors.

CHAPTER TWO

INSPIRATION AND TRACTING

There is a false belief among missionaries that if you tract, you can't do effective member missionary work.

This is absolutely not true! In fact the opposite <u>can</u> be true if you are a great missionary.

You will not sacrifice ANY quality member missionary work if you do it right! The key in this is to do the right kind of work at the right time. I can not emphasize this enough. Do the right work at the right time! All missionary work is not the same value. Let me suggest the order of value of work to bring baptisms.

1. Teaching
2. Member work
3. Contacting Non-members
4. Service work
5. Planning and missionary meetings

Most missionaries don't recognize that different hours and days have different values.

They think that driving to the mission office to pick up a DVD has the same value as teaching a discussion. To them, all work is the same value. This is terribly wrong and cuts your effectiveness as a missionary drastically.

Let me list the most valuable time slots in order.

1. Sunday to Thursday
   6 p.m. to 9 p.m.   non-member finding
2. Saturday & Sunday
   8 a.m. to 6 p.m.   non-member finding

3. Monday to Friday
　　12 a.m. to 6 p.m.　　　all other work
4. Monday to Friday
　　8 a.m. to noon　　　all other work

I call #1 and #2 the Golden Hours. If possible, save these hours for non-member finding because this is when fathers are home!

If possible schedule teaching and all other work in #3 and #4. Remember, members will meet with you when you want in most cases, so you can schedule meeting with them in #3 and #4. If you could teach a discussion in the weekday morning hours, it would be doing the <u>most valuable</u> thing in the <u>least valuable</u> time slot, that is great!

If you have your planning meeting 7 p.m. Sunday, that is terrible! You would be doing the least valuable (and easiest rescheduled) thing in the most valuable time slot.

Analyze each hour often, ask yourself "What is the highest and best use for this hour?"

This one habit will completely change your mission and your life after your mission.

Now let's talk about a special kind of member referral.

THE BEST REFERRAL

Elder Utley, do you believe in member missionaries?"

"Yes, I do."

"Elder Utley, who are the top three members of the Church? I'll give you a clue. Two of them look exactly alike."

"God the Father, Jesus Christ and the Holy Ghost."

"That's right."

"Elder, If these members give you a referral, how good will it be?"

"The best I ever got."

"Yes Elder Utley, a referral from the Lord will be the best. If the Lord tells you which door to knock on, how many doors will you have to knock on?

"Just one!"

I have had that happen. Not very often - but what an experience!

What I am going to tell you next is the only way to have consistent success tracting. All other methods will fail, and are the reason tracting has a bad reputation. This works.

You must ask the Lord unceasingly for inspiration.

RECOGNIZING INSPIRATION (The still small voice method)

How do you know when you receive inspiration from the Lord? This is one of the most important things I will say here today.

You've heard it before, inspiration from the Lord comes in a still, small voice. To make it easier to understand, I like to call it - a hunch. <u>If it is a righteous hunch - do it!</u>

I have talked to leaders of the Church, I've read extensively and even the prophet of the Church said, "The whispering of the spirit comes in a still, small voice." I have found that when I get those hunches, if I try to get them back later, I can't do it. Now, this is very important, <u>when you have a hunch, follow it. Do not doubt yourself!</u> It will not come twice.

FIVE PERSONS ARE READY

Brothers and Sisters, there are <u>five people in your area</u> who are ready to be baptized now, this hour, today! Wherever your area is in your mission, there are five people in your area whom you and your companion can baptize now. I promise you. Next week there will still be five, but they may not be the same five as this week. Do you understand? People move in, and people move out. People have different changes in their lives. Still there is a constant rotation of people that become ready to be harvested. We are sowing seeds on our missions, and some day those seeds will germinate. <u>However, Your calling is to harvest those in your area that are ready and need to be taught and baptized by you.</u> This is how you are going to find them!

PRAY FOR FORGIVENESS

First - you and your companion will kneel down and pray for forgiveness. Repent, Brothers and Sisters. All of us need repentance. Everyone commits sins of commission or omission, even the prophet. Why? Because we all fall short of the Glory of God! I need repentance. Repent of the things that you are doing wrong. <u>Repent of the things you should do that you're not doing</u>.

We are all on different levels. <u>The Lord takes you where you are</u>. He will bless you for your repentance. <u>He does not expect you to be perfect</u> before He cleanses you but <u>He expects you to try</u>. If you will try, <u>even though you are not perfect</u>, He will bless you.

Thank the Lord for the blessings He has given you already. <u>Gratitude is a powerful tool to receive the Spirit. Tell the Lord that you appreciate what He has already given you</u>.

PRAY FOR INSPIRATION

Pray for inspiration. <u>Pray that you will understand the inspiration when it comes</u>. You can even do this prayer for 2:00 in the afternoon, "Father in Heaven, at 2:00 we are going tracting." or "Father in Heaven, at 6:00 we are going tracting." Timing is as important as place. What is the chance that any one of these five people in your area are going to be available where they can hear you and can talk to you at any particular time of day? Pray for your companion. Pray that the Lord will bless him with inspiration.

CHOOSING THE STREETS

After praying for 5 to 15 minutes, one of you take a street map of your area and look over the map. <u>You are looking for streets that you have even a fleeting hunch about. A hunch that is ever so slight</u>. Write it down. You write down 5 to 10 streets. Before you start this process you are asking the Lord, "Father in Heaven, we are going tracting at 10:00 AM today. Who in our area is ready for our message at this time?

TIMING IS IMPORTANT

<u>Timing is as important as place</u>. What is the chance

that any one of these five people in your area will be available, in the spirit and in the mood to hear you and where they can talk to you at any particular time of the day? Maybe not very good. You need to be inspired to visit those people and to knock on their doors at the right time of the day, as well as finding them in the first place. <u>Timing and place are critical for you to meet these people</u>.

THREE TO FIVE STREETS

Pray over the streets, until you have written down five to ten streets. After the list is done, put away the map and <u>both of you look over the list and prayerfully select three to five streets each so that both of you will have a secondary list of streets</u> from this list. <u>You do this individually and then you compare your lists</u>.

Would it surprise you to know that one or two of the streets are the same? I have had as many as three or four the same on each list. How exciting! "Look what we have done, Elder (or Sister). <u>We have put our faith in the Lord for a referral</u>. We have relied on the Spirit. We have exercised our faith and the Lord has given us inspiration."

Enthusiasm is the second most powerful missionary tool!

Then you go out and tract those streets with enthusiasm! If you knock on a door and someone rejects you, you walk away and say, "Well, that wasn't the door. That's not the one we are looking for. That's not the one the Lord sent us to find." But you will have great success as you persevere with faith - and your joy will be great.

TEACHING DISCUSSIONS

You will teach more discussions. <u>You cannot become a great teacher without teaching. It is important to teach a lot of discussions.</u> Discussions are different things in different missions. In our mission a discussion was where you went in, sat down, had a prayer and you taught two or three principles. That was the definition of a "discussion".

Missionaries were teaching three to five discussions a week. After using "inspiration tracting" referrals, we began teaching twelve to eighteen discussions a week. The other elders in my district began to teach that many also, as they followed these steps.

Eventually we were teaching close to twenty discussions a week. The most we ever taught was twenty-six in a week which translates into probably 23 hours a week of teaching experience. That's exciting! By teaching that much, we got to be really good.

It is true that the Lord can use a young, green missionary, and with the power of the Spirit can make him a very effective tool in teaching the gospel through the Spirit of our Father in Heaven. However, It is a lot easier for the Lord to use a polished tool.

You will become polished as you teach more and you will teach more as you tract more. As you tract more, you will receive the blessings the Lord has in store for you because you are working hard. You are relying on the Lord for direction and inspiration.

You are serving the Lord with all your heart, might, mind and strength.

12

USE WARD DIRECTORY FOR REFERRALS

This still, small voice referral method applies to all aspects of missionary work. A powerful example is to use the Ward Directory to find referrals. Ask the Lord to inspire you which members to challenge for referrals by individually praying over the Ward Directory. Select five names each then compare lists. Go to the member's homes and tell them that the Lord inspired you to come to them for referrals. The more you rely on the Lord, the more success you will have. Pray, pray, pray!

Asking for and following specific inspiration is within your reach.

It will be faint and quiet.

He will not repeat it.

If it is a righteous "hunch" --you must do it now.

This is one of the keys to being a great missionary.

CHAPTER THREE

DOOR APPROACHES

Now I want to talk to you about the actual "going up to the door." I imagine many of you are hoping I might give you the "secret door approach" that would get you into each door and guarantee success. There isn't just one, there are hundreds of great door approaches. The secret of being a successful tracting missionary is a combination of 15 to 20 little things. <u>You do all the little things right all of the time and you will be successful</u>.

I am sometimes told, "Elder Marshall, we did the things you said. We prayed and we went out and we knocked on those doors and we didn't meet anybody!"

Does that mean that this doesn't work? Is it possible for you to pray for inspiration and not find anybody to teach?

"Yes, it is possible because those five people in your area may all be busy at that time.

Is the Lord going to tell you "Don't go tracting, Don't work;" or is the Lord going to be pleased that you showed your faith by asking him?

As you show your faith in the Lord by continually praying and asking Him for help, He will bless you.

I gave this seminar last month in Memphis and a few weeks later I ran into a couple of elders. I asked them, "Elders, have you tried the tracting technique?" They said, "We tried it and we didn't meet anybody."

14

I said, "O.K. What about the next time you tried it?" They got this shocked look on their faces, "You mean we should have tried it again?"

<u>Perseverance will overcome your weaknesses</u>. I have weaknesses. I am not a superman, but I have made up for my weaknesses by perseverance and hard work.

So now we are coming to the door approaches: These are some little things that you do as you approach the door. As you and your companion walk up to the house, you are going to <u>look toward the windows</u>. The people inside may see you coming and when they see you looking towards the windows, they may think that you can see them so they will come and answer the door. But if you are talking and looking away and they see that, they may go and hide in the closet. They won't answer the door. You will waste your time and it doesn't give the spirit the opportunity to bear witness to them.

So as I approach the door, I am looking toward the windows and as I step up to the door, I usually knock instead of ringing the doorbell, because you never know if the bell works.

I <u>step up close</u> to the door when I knock, then when the person opens the door, my companion and <u>I step back</u>. This body language tells the people that you expect them to open that second door. (Don't you hate it when they talk through the storm door.)

I don't yell through the door - I talk in a normal voice and I step back a little more as a cue that they are going to open that second door.

15

DOOR APPROACHES

Knock knock.

"Yes, who's there?"

"Hi, how are you today?"

"Fine."

"I am Elder Marshall and this is Elder Kilgore. <u>We are ministers</u> of the Church of Jesus Christ of Latter-day Saints." Notice that I said 'ministers' - and sisters you can call yourself ministers as far as I am concerned, or you can call yourselves "representatives."

You are ministering to these people and a lot of these people have ministers in their churches as young as you are. They understand that better than if you say "missionaries". Some people have strange ideas when you say "missionaries". So we are ministers of the Church of Jesus Christ of Latter-day Saints.

<u>I speak slowly and distinctly and look into their eyes.</u> Brothers and Sisters, they should see Christ at their door. You will be looking them in the eye and the Spirit will convey to them through your eyes that you are from the Lord. If you saw the Savior a hundred yards away - would you recognize him? You might or you might not. Many people would not recognize the Savior if they saw him 100 yards away, but if the Savior were standing three feet away and looking into your eyes, would you recognize him then? Virtually everyone would recognize the Savior if he were standing in front of them and looking into their eyes. <u>You are representa-</u>

tives of the Savior and the people can feel His spirit through you at the door.

That's why we want these people to come to the door so they can have this opportunity. If they are hiding in the closet, they are going to miss that opportunity, and you have wasted two or three minutes of your mission.

Now back to the door approach. "Have you ever known any Mormons?" (I like to say the second name of the Church.) Do you know any Mormons? I hate it when people slam the door in my face because they think I'm a Jehovah's Witness. I want them to know who they are rejecting so I give them both names of the Church in my presentation.

Lady of the house: "Yes, I have known a few but I have my own church."

"We understand that you have your own church but would you be interested in learning about this church for your own information?"

"No, I think I know all about your church."

"Well, you have a good day."

I give them two opportunities to reject me. I want them to reject me twice to make sure they are not the one that I'm looking for and I want to leave with a positive impression. Smile and say, "Have a nice day." Then quickly depart and go to the next door with enthusiasm because that next door might be the one to which the Lord sent you. Let's try the next door.

Knock, Knock.

"Hello"

"Hi, how are you today?"

"Fine."

"Great. I am Elder Marshall and this is Elder Kilgore, we are ministers of the Church of Jesus Christ of Latter-day Saints. Have you ever known any Mormons?"

"No."

"Great! We have an exciting message. Can we visit with you?"

"I'm too busy today. I've got too much to do."

(I want to emphasize that we are trying to teach here and now. I want to get in and teach this person now so I try to take a direct approach and hope they won't think of a reason not to let us in. So she's too busy. How many times do you hear that? She has to get back to the "soap opera". Now I need to find out if she really is too busy or is she just trying to get rid of me?) So I ask "Would you be interested if we came back another time?"

"I don't know."

"Would you like us to take your number and give you a call?" (We are always going to get her <u>name and</u>

18

<u>phone number</u> so we can call and confirm our appointment especially if we feel she may not meet with us. This saves a lot of the Lord's time.)

"I don't think so."

"OK. Thank you very much. You have a good day."

When you come to the door and sometimes they just open it a crack and say, "I'm really very busy. I don't have time to talk to you." Early in my mission I would start talking real fast because they were so busy and they would slam the door, but here is what you do instead. Speak clearly and say, "Oh, I understand. We'll be really brief." <u>Then you talk as slowly as you want</u>. Deliver your message and say that you will come back another time. They will stand there and listen to you <u>because you have acknowledged their objection.</u>

By using these techniques I very rarely had doors slammed in my face. They were shut slowly, which makes it nicer for you if nothing else and it does give the Spirit an opportunity to testify to them. Sometimes with wonderful results.

Have you ever gone up to a solid door, no window, just a solid door, and you knock and you hear a voice on the other side that asks, "Who is it!?" That used to frustrate me! How do you give a "door approach" through a solid door? Then I found the secret. When you hear "Who is it?"

Simply answer, "It's US!" Now they just HAVE to see who "US" is! It almost never failed.

CHAPTER FOUR

TWO CHOICE DECISIONS
Knock, knock

"Hello."

"I am Elder Marshall and this is Elder Kilgore. We are ministers of the Church of Jesus Christ of Latter-day Saints. Do you know any Mormons?"

"No."

"We have an exciting message. Can we visit with you?"

"I don't have time right now."

"Would you be interested if we came back another time?"

"That would be better."

"Would today or tomorrow be better?"

"Tomorrow would be better."

This is the "commitment portion" to your door approach. This is where you commit this person to an appointment and you need to make it easy for them.

People like to have simple decisions. We call this "Two Choice Decision". I'm going to give her <u>two choices</u> for every decision that she needs to make and we will quickly set an appointment.

First I asked: "Would today or tomorrow be better?" (Two choices)

"Today"

"Would during the day or during the evening be better?" (Two choices)

"Probably during the evening."

"Would 7:00 or 8:30 be better?" (Two choices)

"I believe 8:30 p.m. would be better."

We would take her name and phone number. If we have a lot of appointments, we would call her to make sure she was going to keep that appointment. Many times people will give you an appointment and may not have any intention of keeping it. Or perhaps other things will happen. So if you go over there and they aren't there, then you have wasted the Lords time. So call first.

DOUBLE BOOKING

When things are really busy and we have a lot of appointments, I even "double-book", make several appointments for the same time - and tell them ....

"We may have to call and confirm this, but would 7:00 be alright?" Then if I had two or three at 7:00 I would call the first one and say "We are coming over. They might say, "We can't make it" or "We're not interested." The second one might say, "OK, we'll be ready."

21

Then I would call the third one and say, "We can't make it at 7:00 o'clock. Can we re-schedule?" In doing that, we were able to teach two discussions a night.

TIMES USAGE: 7:00 and 8:30 CRITICAL HOURS

Seven o'clock and 8:30 are critical. You cannot teach two discussions a night if you make your appointments at any other time than 7:00 and 8:30. I've tried it - it can't be done. And if possible <u>you need to fill your 8:30 appointments first</u> - why? Because if you get a 7:00 appointment and your 8:30 doesn't hold - you're done! You don't have time to do anything else that evening, and like I said, we want to teach two discussions every night. In fact, hopefully you will have members splitting with you so you and your companion are both out on "splits" and you will be teaching four discussions each evening.

THE GOLDEN HOURS

Evening hours are Golden! The time of the day, from <u>6:00 on is worth more for</u> <u>missionary work than</u> <u>the whole rest of the day.</u>

Tracting in the morning when everybody is at work, and in the afternoon is very difficult. Not that you shouldn't do it, because you should. You should exercise your faith in the Lord and show him that you are serious about working hard all the time. <u>But treasure the evening hours.</u> Don't let anything rob the Lord of those evening hours.

What about Saturdays? <u>Saturdays are as valuable as the evening hours.</u> All day Saturday is a fabulous time to be out preaching the gospel and meeting people.

What about Sundays? <u>Sundays are even better!</u> Sundays are perhaps the best day of the week to tell people about the Lord. I treasured my Sundays. I rarely took dinner appointments on Sunday because I wanted to be out sharing the gospel with the people when they were receptive.

One elder said to me, "Well, you know, Elder Marshall, when we are tracting between 5:00 and 7:00 in the evening - people are eating and they come to the door and they are bothered because we have interrupted their meal." Baloney! Don't give a thought to that, Brothers and Sisters. Do not avoid tracting around dinner hours because no matter when you tract, people will be eating. If it's 8:00 at night or 3:00 in the afternoon, there will be people eating.

Your message is so important that you need to deliver it to those people as you are inspired and when they are home. Those that are ready will be touched by the Spirit. Even if they are in the middle of dinner, they will look into your eyes and see the Saviour standing there. They will be touched and they will be receptive. So be bold. <u>Do not fear that you will interrupt someone's dinner.</u>

CHAPTER FIVE

TEACHING WHILE TRACTING

Knock, knock

"Hello"

"I am Elder Marshall and this is Elder Kilgore. We are ministers of the Church of Jesus Christ of Latter-day Saints. Have you ever known any Mormons?"

"Yes, I worked with a Mormon once."

"Great! We have an exciting message about Jesus Christ to share with you. May we visit with you?"

"Right now?"

"Yes!"

"O.K."

She said "<u>Yes</u>" so we are going to teach her <u>right now</u> (As long as she's not alone). As we walk into the home we check things out. We want to have a good teaching environment. I like to sit around a table if possible. It's not the only answer but I just like to sit around a table. If there is no table and there is a sofa and some chairs, I like the two missionaries to sit together.

We need the radio and television turned off so I would say something like this after thanking her for inviting us in.

"Since we are going to discuss religion <u>we would like to start with a prayer, would it be alright to turn off the television</u>?"

FIND OUT WHO YOU ARE TEACHING
The first thing you do after you get in the door is find out who you are talking to. Who is this person?

"And your name is?"

"Mrs. Whiteway."

"Well, Mrs. Whiteway, do you have a church you are attending?"

"Yes, I have. I attend the Belleview Baptist Church.

"That's wonderful. Are you active in your church?"

"Yes. I've been 'born again.'"

WHAT DOES SHE BELIEVE?
Now, what I'm going to do is find out <u>who this person</u> is before I teach her, because I'm going to teach Mrs. Whiteway with different things than I would an atheist or a Buddhist or an inactive member. One of the questions I'm going to ask is:

"Do you believe the Bible is the Word of God?"

"Oh, I do. I read it every day, very faithfully."

Now I know that she believes in the Bible. Many

25

people do not believe in the Bible and if you ask a few questions about their belief in the Bible you may find out that they think it was written by some old men and has no real relevance today. If that's true, then there's not much point in quoting verses out of the scriptures while you are teaching them.

ASK QUESTIONS

The Lord expects you - not only to be inspired, but to use your brain and to ask questions. Find out who you are teaching. Let the Spirit guide you as to what to teach. <u>You should have a variety of discussions that you can teach people so the Spirit can direct you,</u> "I think I'll teach this discussion to this person." If you have only one possible discussion to teach people when you get in, how can the spirit direct you to teach them anything else? So I have developed a number of discussions.

DISCUSSIONS SHOULD BE BRIEF

It is important to be brief in your discussions. I believe that no discussion should go more than 45 minutes. Do I do that? Well, I try to. A lot of the time if I shoot for 45 minutes, I end up with an hour. You want people to want you to come back. If you sit there in their living room and talk to them for two hours, even though they seem to be enjoying it and the spirit is there, they may think, "Gee, I don't know if I want them to come back. I don't have another two hours to spend with them."

LEAVE THEM WANTING MORE

But if you shoot for one-half hour or 45 minutes in your teaching, no matter which discussion you teach, you leave them wanting more - wanting you to come back.

"Gosh, do you have to leave so soon?"
They are anxious for you to return.

Now, to get back to Mrs. Whiteway. We have found out that she is a Belleview Baptist. We know Belleview Baptist Church is famous for educating its members about cults, so I know who I'm talking to here. My hunch (inspiration) on this is that I'm going to teach her "Christ in America" and the Book of Mormon. This is my favorite first discussion.

THREE PART MESSAGE

I want to leave these people with three things. In fact it's a good idea to say, "We're going to tell you three things. We are going to tell you that Jesus is the Christ, that He has restored His Church and how you can know that it is true. This is our message."

As missionaries what is your message? This is it! You are trying to help them to have a testimony that the Church has been restored so they will join the Lord's Church. I would come in and talk to Mrs. Whiteway, pull out my Book of Mormon - which brings up another thing - I carry my Book of Mormon in my belt behind my back and my companion has one also. We would never have more than two with us when we went tracting until we get back to our bikes or car.

Early in my mission I decided that I would do away with the big scriptures during tracting so I got a pocket size New Testament. Between the Book of Mormon and the New Testament I found that I was able to answer almost any question that might come up. If there were more questions than that, people usually have an Old Testament in their home.

What did that do? It let me walk up to the door with my hands free. With this hot weather we have here in the South, it's nice not to have to carry around a bunch of stuff with you. Also when you walk up to the door you don't look like a book salesman. I feel it is less intimidating to people and they are more willing to let you in.

So-- No books, no backpack. We would leave two extra Book of Mormons on the bikes, that was enough. (You can leave them on the bike, they won't get stolen.)

When the Jehovah's Witness come to my door, they have this stack of books with them and they want to come in and talk to me - I think "I'm not ready for this." Even though I am who I am, there's something intimidating about them carrying a load of books into my house. No big deal though if you like to carry your scriptures - most missionaries do, I'm just saying that this is just another little thing that I learned.

As I was saying, you have the New Testament in your shirt pocket and the Book of Mormon behind your back and we come in the house and we pull out the Book of Mormon. We turn to the picture of Christ descending in America. We teach them about that and we talk about the Book of Mormon. One of the first things that comes up in discussions is "We have the Bible, why do we need anything more?"

The Book of Mormon does <u>two things that the Bible cannot do:</u> It's a second testament that <u>Jesus is the Christ</u>

and it is a tool the Lord has given us so we can know whether or not Joseph Smith is a true prophet.

ONLY TRUE OR FALSE PROPHETS

There is an interesting thing about prophets: There are only <u>true prophets</u> and <u>false prophets.</u> There is nothing in between. Joseph Smith was either a true prophet or he was a false prophet. The Book of Mormon is the word of God - or it is not. <u>If the Book of Mormon is the word of God, then Joseph Smith was a true prophet </u>and the <u>Church of Jesus Christ of Latter-day Saints is the Lord's Church</u> here on the earth. It is as simple as ABC. If you can establish that to a person <u>intellectually</u>, they will have the desire to pray to learn it <u>spiritually</u>. If you have not already given them the spiritual experience in your presentation.

The next thing we want to talk about is getting people to church. There are major hurdles that people have to cross on their way to baptism and <u>you should take great victory</u> when you cross one of these hurdles.

One of the hurdles is that they pray.

Another is that they read.

A very large one is that they come out to church.

I have known people who believe that the Church is true and have visited with the missionaries for years but they would never come out to church. Can you baptize them? No.

On the other hand I have known people who have

come out to church after just one invitation, and not knowing what to expect, found that they liked it because they had a positive experience. When they were taught, they already knew that we were not a "bunch of crazies".

INVITING PEOPLE TO CHURCH

You need to get your people to church. I would suggest that you write down the time of our meetings so you can give these to your people and encourage the members to remind their friends. In fact, you can ask a prospective missionary or your ward mission leader to call each member, including children, and ask them one simple question, "Do you know anyone you could invite to church next week?" Some will say "Yes" each week! The members will think you're great!

What kind of problems have you had getting people to come to church?

Sister Missionary: "They are afraid of the unknown."

Aren't we all afraid of the unknown? One of the things we would do is to invite them to church on a week night or a Saturday and we would show off the facilities. In most areas we have nice facilities. We would bring them in and show them where they were going to enter. We show them the chapel, where they were going to sit and show them the cultural hall and the library. We would talk about the genealogy program of the church and show them the baptism area. It makes them feel more at ease.

WHEN DO YOU CALL?

When do you call people to invite them to church? There are two times that you call people. First you call them on <u>Saturday night</u>. Then you call them the <u>next morning</u>. What time do you call them in the morning? <u>Two hours before meeting time</u>. If they are called only one hour ahead they would not have time to get ready and be to church on time.

Make up some excuse to wake them up "Oh, I forgot to tell you, we are going to have a special speaker. "Little Suzie is going to tell about ....." because if you don't "the alarm didn't work" or there will be some other problem and they won't show up. I repeat, you must call 1 1/2 to two hours before services. If at all possible, see if you can get the investigator to ride with a member. Tell them "We'll have the Brown's come over and pick you up." You might have the investigator come and pick you up. One of the things Elders on bikes would say is, "We don't have a ride to church, could you possibly give us a ride?"

If the investigator is giving you a ride to church, they have made a commitment and someone else is depending on them. They virtually always come. Getting people to church is of critical importance. The people who come to church are, to you, the most important people on the face of the earth. They are more important than if the Prophet himself, would come.

(Asking a Missionary Sister): Let us suppose that President Monson is coming to church this Sunday, I would like you to be sure that he has a good experience. Would that be exciting? "Would you be enthused about

31

him coming?"

"Yes, I would."

When he came in, would you be standing in the foyer talking to some young men? When he got there would you say "Hi, Prophet. They are meeting in there, Prophet. Just go on in and make yourself comfortable."?

"Probably not."

"What would you do?"

"I would be with him all the time."

STAY WITH YOUR INVESTIGATORS

Brothers and Sisters, your investigators are more important to you than a visit from the Prophet. <u>Stay with your investigators every second</u>. If they bring children, <u>you must make these children have a good experience</u>. You may have to recruit some members of the church to help you with the children. When the children go to class, a missionary will go with them. Why? What happens if the child gets in class and little Susie punches him? It happens!

You want the children to have a wonderful experience. You want to love the children. Show enthusiasm for the investigator's children and show enthusiasm for the member's children. <u>People love people that love their children</u> and if you love the children, you will impress the parents.

WHAT IF THEY ARE LATE?

Now here's a scenario: Your investigators are late

and they pull into the parking lot. Services have already started and they are singing the opening song. Are you in the chapel sitting behind closed doors? No. You're still out in the foyer, one on each side of the building because you're not sure which door they will enter. You are watching for your investigators.

So the opening song has begun and the investigators pull up outside. You signal your companion. You go running out to them, "Oh, we are so glad you could make it. Come on in."

So they come in and the doors are shut. The congregation is singing and everybody is seated inside. Your investigators say, "Oh gee, have they already started?" You say, "Oh, that's all right."

FRONT AND CENTER

Your companion has been tipped off that the investigators are there. By pre-arrangement he has swung into action. He has come into the chapel and gone up to the second or third row and has moved the members apart and cleared a spot right in front and center.

We are going to sit our investigators right up front. Why? Because that's where they will have the best experience. If you let them sit in the back - who's sitting in the back? Teenagers. They are wonderful, but they go out on Saturday night and need to whisper a little bit about what they were doing, causing a little disruption. Young children and mothers with disruptive children sometimes are in the back. It's just not as good to have your investigators sit in the back. Have your investigators sit up front.

What does it do to have your investigators sit up front and center? What happens if the sound system doesn't work? Do all the sound systems in all of our buildings work all the time? They usually work - but if they are sitting in the back and the sound system doesn't work right, they aren't going to be able to hear. However, if they are up front, they don't need the sound system because they will be able to hear and they will have a positive experience. They will be able to feel the speaker's spirit more easily.

There is another thing it does - Elder Utley, go down and stand by that third row. OK, now look at that back door - put your hand up like you are motioning for the investigator to come sit up front. Now when I open the door with my investigators they will say, "Oh gee, they have already started. We'll sit in the back."

"No, look, there's Elder Utley. He's saved a spot for us." I bring the investigators right up and Elder Utley ushers them in. Do the Ward members see this? Yes! And they are thinking, "Look at those missionaries bringing in more investigators to learn about the gospel. What great missionaries we have!" You are advertising to the whole ward, what enthusiastic and great missionaries you are.

Brothers and sisters, <u>you need to build your</u> <u>reputation among the members.</u> You can take this goal by the hand and do it yourself. You need to elevate your reputation with the ward members and you can do that.

Why do you want to have a good reputation with the

members? Because they will give you referrals! Are the members likely to give referrals to missionaries they don't respect? Are members enthusiastic to share their friends. Who they have been working on for years with a great missionary?

How do they know you are a 'great' missionary? The answer: <u>They see you in action</u>. Show them your best all the time!

We have already told these people what to expect in our services. While we are in the service, we are sitting with them, we are whispering, quietly making comments about what is going on in the service. "Notice over here the young men are blessing the sacrament. In the Lord's church we believe it is important for the young people to have an active part in the church, so the Lord has arranged that they can have the priesthood at an early age and have an active part." You share little things like this and different comments about the speakers. I might say, "One of the great things about our church is: If you don't like the speaker, just wait 10 minutes and there will be a new one."

CHAPTER SIX

CREATING MEMBER FELLOWSHIPPING

Brothers and sisters, <u>share your experiences with the members</u>. In each of your areas there are some members more 'fired up' than other members. You need to <u>identify</u> those as soon as possible and share with them the experiences you have at church or even call them at their home. This is one of the keys to my success in tracting. Tracting has not been successful for many missionaries in the church because there hasn't been the tie-in with the social structure of the church.

When you do member missionary work, the people being baptized have a connection - they know the members. When you are tracting and bring in somebody new, they don't have that social connection. <u>You are going to forge that social connection yourself</u>, and here is how you are going to do it.

You are out tracting and you meet the Smith family. You have a great discussion with them and challenge them to come to church. You and your companion think about all the people you know in the ward and you say, "I think the Marshalls would be best suited because they are about the same age and they have kids of the same age. Let's use the Marshalls for the "fellowshipping family" for the people we have just tracted out."

We call up Sister Marshall and say, "Sister Marshall, we just had the greatest experience today. We knelt down and prayed to our Father in Heaven where we should go tracting and we were inspired that we should go over to Maple Street and tract there. When we got there we met this wonderful family - the Smiths. They invited us in, and we taught the gospel to them. The Spirit was so strong, it was almost as if there was an Angel there and they accepted our challenge to come to Church."

"We are wondering if you could come a little bit early and sit up in the third row center and help us fellowship them and meet them. Could you do that?" What is Sister Marshall going to say except - "I'll do it!"

WHAT, WHEN AND HOW

You are going to tell the members <u>What to do, when to do it and how to do it</u>. You are going to check back on them to make sure that they do it, <u>in a loving way</u>. The members want to help you. They want to further the Lord's work as much as you do, but they don't know how. You are the experts! You know the needs of your investigators so you are going to <u>tell the members exactly what to do</u> (<u>you must be Christ-like in doing this</u>).

Choose the members that you want to do it. You are going to tell them what to do and you are going to hold their hand through the whole process. The members of the Church are just like everybody else. They are caught up in their daily affairs and a lot of the time they don't plan on what they need to do. They want to do what's right, but they really don't know how. If you will hold their hand and help them to do it, they will have a great experience. They will love you for it and your reputation will build tremendously.

Have any of you had experience with "the Mormon grapevine"? The Mormon grapevine can be a powerful resource. How are we going to use it? We are going to use it as a powerful tool for good.

Sister Marshall hangs up the phone after talking to the Elder about the spiritual experience with the Smith family. She then picks up the phone and calls Sister Turley and says: "Elder Utley was telling me about this great family he met. He and his companion prayed about where to go and the Lord told them the exact street."

They went there and they met the Smith family who are coming to church Sunday. While they were teaching the discussion, angels appeared in the room! Then Sister Turley calls Sister Nelson and suddenly there are two or three legions of angels in the room. Well, by the time Sunday comes around, <u>you are Moses</u>! You <u>can</u> build your reputation in the Ward. You <u>need</u> to build your reputation in the Ward.

BIRD-DOGGING

What if your investigators arrive on time before the services begin, you go out to the car to pick them up. Your companion is running around in the foyer grabbing people and saying, "Listen, my companion is bringing in a new family that we just met while tracting. Would you please introduce yourselves to them?" We are making sure that our investigators have a positive experience. We call this "bird dogging". We are telling the members what to do and when to do it, and they will love you for it! You are also building your reputation.

Sister Marshall, would you come up here, please? The first time you came to church, tell about your experience.

38

Sister Marshall: "The first time I went to church I was overwhelmed. Elder Marshall stayed with me while Elder Harris went around to every family that was at church and people were backed up in the foyer greeting me. They made me feel very welcome. Recently I went to Birmingham, Alabama visiting some old friends and an old boyfriend wanted me to go to a "drag race" one Saturday night. I said I would go if he would go to church with me on Sunday morning. I had already talked to the missionaries before going down there."

"They knew me and knew that I was coming and was going to bring some people with me so they went around and got members to come over and greet them to make sure they knew that they were welcome. It's really important to know that someone, other than the missionaries, cares that you are there."

Brother Marshall:

The ward that I was in had the reputation of having the "greatest members in the entire mission." It wasn't true. They weren't the greatest members in the entire mission. They were no better members than in all the other wards, but my companions and the other companions in my district practiced these things that I am telling you and we had tremendous member involvement. When our tracting baptisms did occur, <u>we had the chapel full during the baptisms</u>. We had forged that bond between members and our new converts so if we were transferred they were not left high and dry to fall away.

As you may know it's a problem when missionaries develop a great bond with their converts and they baptize them. Then the missionaries are transferred out. The new converts feel they are forgotten. Sometimes the people go inactive. That doesn't need to happen if the missionaries do the proper work in making sure the members fellowship.

Another thing, Let's say you didn't have any investigators show up at the church. What should you be doing? Well, one thing I did was stand at the back door and watch for investigators through the whole service. I would also stand back there, look at the members in the Ward and try to remember their names. I would make notes on which ones would be good for certain types of investigators. I would make notes of which ones I was going to talk to after services.

MEMBER MISSIONARY WORK

Member missionary work is important. You can do the most effective missionary work at church. You can visit more members at church in a shorter period of time than you could in many hours through the week. You've got them all right there. They are all dressed up. They are in a spiritual mood and if you work effectively, you can go around before church and after church, talk to different families and ask, "Hey, have you got any friends that you could invite to church?" Be sure to write down the names they mention so you can follow up on them.

TEENAGERS

And what about the teenagers? The teenagers are the best about inviting their friends to church. My kids have brought more non-members to church than I have this last year. Even the Primary is a great source of invitations to visit Church. We cannot emphasize enough the importance of not wasting the Lord's time. One way to do that is by utilizing your hours on Sunday to their maximum value. Do not spend too much time with one member or member family. Keep working. <u>Sunday is not a day of rest for the missionaries</u>.

CHALLENGE THE MEMBERS

Challenge them. It will build your reputation as a hard-working servant of the Lord. Remember when I talked about major goals and obstacles in getting someone baptized? When you get somebody to church - you have accomplished a major goal and a great accomplishment. <u>You should take great joy in it!</u>

So challenge the members to invite their friends to church. It will be a great joy for them, too.

Write down the names of their friends. Keep a notebook. Keep track of all this. Then follow up to make sure they do invite their friends.

Share with your members how their investigators are coming along. Continue to forge that link. Tell your members <u>what to do, when</u> to do it and how it do it.

<u>If it was appropriate</u>, I have said things like: "Sister Brown, could you take a loaf of bread over to Sister Smith this Tuesday night and just tell her how much you appreciate her. You know she has been feeling "down". Tell her how much you appreciate her coming to church. You are telling Sister Brown what to do, when to do it and how to do it. Then you can check back and say, "Have you had a chance to do that yet? We are so excited, we wondered what her reaction was when you took that loaf of bread over to her."

41

MULTIPLE FAMILIES

Question from the floor: "What if you have two families come to Church the same Sunday?"

I'm so glad you asked that. At the height of our success, on one occasion, we had five families at church at one time. First of all, if you see another missionary needing help, you need to be in there doing everything you can to help those other missionaries. If there are not multiple missionaries in the Ward, then you should have pre-arranged with key members to help you. Have them do the bird-dogging, and go to the different Sunday School classes with the children.

In Memphis, a Sister Lesueur was wonderful to me. One Sunday I brought a lady with her two little children to church and Sister Lesueur and her companion loved those two little kids, took them to Primary, and when they came out of Primary I had their mother with me. The kids gave Sister Lesueur a kiss on the cheek, and for a week after that they wanted to know when they could go back to "that church"? I really appreciate Sister Lesueur for that. The members will love you when you give them an opportunity to share the gospel. They will respect you, they will love you and they will do anything for you.

It is important to arrive at church at least 30 minutes early. You should split up with qualified members to cover both doors of the church to greet everyone and to spot non-members. This is also another way to boost your reputation!

You should remain in the foyer until _after_ the

Sacrament is passed. Yes, it is nicer to sit inside with the congregation, but you cannot see late investigators arrive from there, and they leave unnoticed because the doors are shut. Your bet chance to do missionary work during the passing of the sacrament, is to be where you can greet late arriving non-members. Of course you still get to take the sacrament in the foyer. Now obviously, if you don't have good fellowship families to sit with your investigators, then you need to be inside sitting with them. This is another example of using every minute of your mission to its highest value. I want to emphasize again that you need to constantly share short uplifting stories about teaching your investigators. When a member asks you how you are, don't say "Fine", say "Great, we had the best discussion with the Smith family, ..." then talk for 3 to 5 minutes about how spiritual it was. This is what members want to hear from their missionaries. Also, it builds your reputation as a great missionary that they can trust with their referrals.

IMPORTANT TIP

Before Church starts, <u>ask the Bishop and both his counselors to shake hands with your investigators every Sunday without fail</u>. They will follow through, even if no one else will, and it is <u>impressive</u> to visitors. This would also help <u>retention</u> of new converts and inactive members.

TEACH THEM HOW TO PRAY

When you start teaching people you need to get them to pray. Teaching a non-member how to pray is always a challenge and an important one of those hurdles. On your flip charts are the steps to a prayer. I would scribble them down on a piece of paper and give to the investigator so they would have them to use during a prayer. I would say, "Just hold it down here like this." It would make it easier for them to pray. They could teach their children how to pray and also, have something to review.

Four Steps to Prayer

1. Our Heavenly Father
2. We thank Thee ....
3. We ask Thee .....
4. In the name of Jesus Christ. Amen.

CHAPTER SEVEN

FRUITS CARDS - The Fruits of the Church

I got to thinking one day that I should get some cards printed up with the steps of a prayer on it. Then I realized that the other side of the card would be blank. I had been reading "A Marvelous Work and a Wonder" and it talks about the fruits of the church, so we put the "fruits" of the Church on the other side. We call these "fruits cards".

"In Reference to Prophets"
Matthew 7:15 - 20

The Lord said in the Sermon on the Mount: "A good tree cannot bring forth evil fruit, neither can a corrupt tree bring forth good fruit ... Wherefore by their fruits ye shall know them."

A FEW OF THE FRUITS OF THE CHURCH OF JESUS CHRIST OF LATTER-DAY SAINTS.

1. Emphasis on faith in Jesus Christ.
2. Specific programs to build strong families.
3. Leader in Youth Development.
4. Most people per capita in Who's Who in U.S.
5. Least number of divorces per capita.
6. Highest number of college graduates per capita.
7. Lowest death rate per capita.
8. Highest birth rate per capita.
9. Lowest cancer rate per capita.
10. Highest educational standards.
11. Largest and oldest women's organization in U.S.
12. Highest health code.
13. Most efficient welfare plan.
14. Unpaid ministry.
15. Fastest growing Church.

Was Joseph Smith a Prophet: James 1:5

Permission granted to reprint.

These are great missionary tools. You can teach your investigators how to pray. Then you can teach the discussion about the fruits of the church and leave it with them so they can reflect on it.

Seventeen Characteristics of the True Church.

The True Church:

1. Was organized by Jesus Christ. *Ephesians 4:10-16*
2. Bears the name of Jesus Christ. *1 Corinthians 6:11*
3. Has a foundation of apostles and prophets. *Ephesians 2:19-20*
4. Has the same organization as Jesus Christ's Church. *Ephesians 4:11-16*
5. Claims divine authority. *Hebrews 5:4-6*
6. Has no paid ministry. *1 Thessalonians 2:9; Acts 20:33-35*
7. Baptizes by immersion. *Matthew 3:13-17*
8. Bestows the gift of the Holy Ghost by the laying on of hands. *Acts 8:14-17*
9. Practices divine healing. *Mark 3:14-15*
10. Teaches that Heavenly Father and Jesus Christ are separate and distinct individuals. *John 17:11; 20:17*
11. Teaches that Heavenly Father and Jesus Christ have bodies of flesh and bones. *Luke 24:33-34; 36-39; Genesis 5:1*
12. Has its officers called by God. *Exodus 40:13-16; Hebrews 5:4*
13. Claims revelation from God. *Amos 3:7*
14. Is a missionary church. *Matthew 28:19-20*
15. Is a restored church. *Acts 3:19-21*
16. Practices baptism for the dead. *1 Corinthians 15:3-4,20-22,29*
17. By their fruits ye shall know them. *Matthew 5:16; Titus 3:8*

Why are these things important? *Hebrews 13:8*

- Bible: KJV

TRUE AND FALSE PROPHETS

We would teach our investigators right out of the scriptures. I talked earlier about there are only true prophets and false prophets. In the New Testament the Lord addresses this question. In Matthew 7:15-20. It is interesting that the <u>Lord didn't say, "There will be no more prophets</u>". Many churches teach that there are no more prophets. Well, if there are to be no more prophets, the Lord would have said, "Hey, there are no more prophets and if anybody says there are - then they are a false prophet."

Instead, He says in verse fifteen, "Beware of false prophets which come to you in sheep's clothing, but inwardly they are ravening wolves." <u>And then he tells us how we can know if they are false or true prophets</u>. Sometimes people will use this scripture to justify organizations or groups of people or teachers. But this does not apply to organizations or other churches.

<u>The Lord here speaks specifically about prophets</u> and he is not talking about a teacher. For instance, Billy Graham does not have to live to this standard because he doesn't claim to be a prophet. Jimmy Swagart and Jim Baker don't have to live by this standard even though some of the things they taught were good and some were evil.

But Joseph Smith and the fourteen other prophets we have had, must live by the standard, <u>for they are either true prophets, or they are false prophets</u>. How do you know if they are true prophets or false prophets?

BY THEIR FRUITS ....

Matthew 7:16 "<u>Ye shall know them by their fruits</u>."

What are their fruits? I suggest their fruits are the things they produce. "Do men gather grapes of thorns and figs of thistle? Even so every good tree bringeth forth good fruit; but a corrupt tree bringeth forth evil fruit." "A good tree cannot bring forth evil fruit, <u>neither can a corrupt tree bring forth good fruit</u>."

Brothers and sisters, the Lord is comparing a prophet to a tree, would you not agree? He goes so far as to say that a corrupt tree cannot bring forth good fruit.

The Church of Jesus Christ of Latter-day Saints is the Lord's Church. It is a church that has been directed by a prophet, was founded by a modern prophet and there would be either an <u>abundance of good fruit in the church or of corrupt fruit</u>, and I want to testify to you that in all my years of association with the Church I have never seen anything corrupt in the teachings of the Church. There may be a corrupt person here or there but the teachings of the Church and the things that the Church is trying to do are as pure as the Lord himself.

So we would point that out and we would say, "Let's go through a few of the fruits of the Church, Brother Brown. Here are a few of the fruits of Joseph Smith and the fourteen prophets that have followed him:

#1 - Emphasis on faith in Jesus Christ. Would you say that teaching that Jesus Christ is our Saviour is a good fruit or bad fruit?

"Gee, that sounds like a great fruit to me!"

#2 - Specific programs to help build strong families.

"Brother Brown, the Lord has revealed to us through the prophets that we are here in families for a sacred purpose. God has placed us here in families because He wants us to teach each other about Him and to return to Him as a family unit."

"Brother Brown, would you say that strong families is a good fruit or a bad fruit?"

"It's a good fruit."

#3 - Leaders in youth development

#4 - Most people per capita in Who's Who.

#5 - Least number of divorces per capita.

#6 - A high number of college graduates per capita.

These are things that are brought about by the Lord's emphasis on serving our fellowman. And in education: the glory of God is intelligence. The Lord has told us that we must learn as much as we can. The natural by-products of these things are the things that we have listed here.

#7 - Lowest death rate per capita. Highest birth rate per capita. The Lord has given us His wisdom on how to have a healthier and happier life. We call it the Word of Wisdom and it has brought forth health and happiness. Are these good fruits or bad fruits?

"Why Elder Marshall, I think those are good fruits." Now some of these are a little bit redundant but they give you an opportunity to talk about the many blessings that come from being a member of the Church.

#13 - Most efficient welfare plan. The Lords Church has a world famous plan to take care of the needy.

AN UNPAID MINISTRY
#14 - An unpaid ministry: What a refreshing concept! The Lord wants us to serve one another for love NOT money. We have NO collection plates and when we donate in secret, we know the money is not buying a fur coat for the bishop's wife. The way the Church handles money is nothing less than inspired.

Was Joseph Smith a prophet? What did the fruits say? It's a powerful argument. These cards are also great for talking to the members. You can present these to the members and teach them how to teach their friends. They may not be able to teach their friends about Joseph Smith and the Golden Bible but they can bear testimony of what the Church has done for them in their lives.

Every good member of the Church has a strong testimony of the blessings of the gospel and how it has changed their lives. That is what people want. People want to know what the Church can do for them. The Church can do more for them than any organization on earth. I know it and I feel that you know it.

Sister Marshall, Elder Esplin and Elder Knudsen and

I were teaching a part-member family, a young man, about the Church, I think what convinced him was that <u>we have all the good things in the Church that he could find in any other religion</u>. He kept saying, "Well, I'm a Methodist. I was born a Methodist." I kept asking him, "Tell me something in the Methodist Church that is good that we don't have in the Mormon Church." He was speechless. Finally he said, "Well, there is nothing."

I said, "Then you agree that we have all the good things that are in the Methodist Church?"

He said, "Yes."

It was an important step on his way to being baptized.

When you are teaching discussions, <u>don't bog down on disagreements</u>. If your investigator has an issue with a teaching in the Church, try to avoid it and move on to the most important things that you are trying to teach.

The most important things that you are trying to teach are that <u>Jesus is the Christ</u>, (hopefully they already know this), that <u>Joseph Smith was used by the Lord to restore His church</u> and <u>how they can know this is true through the Book of Mormon</u>. Like we talked about prophets, the Book of Mormon is either the Word of God or it is a fraud. The sooner you can establish that - the better off your investigator will be.

<u>Your investigator is not going to pay any attention to the teachings of the Church until he has a testimony</u>. That is: A testimony that Joseph Smith was a true

prophet. - Sometimes people accuse us of talking too much about Joseph Smith. Sometimes they might be right. We should put Jesus Christ in front of Joseph Smith, such as, "We testify that Jesus Christ used Joseph Smith to restore the Church" rather than saying "Joseph Smith restored the Church."

The fact is that a testimony of Jesus Christ using Joseph Smith to restore the Church is the turning point. What happens when you ask your investigator, "Was Joseph Smith a true prophet?", and he says "Yes".

Fill the font! If Joseph Smith is a true prophet and the Church of Jesus Christ is here upon the earth today, and he says, "Yes", He is ready for the commandments. I remember one of our investigators that we had just started teaching asked, "What's this I hear about Mormons don't drink tea and don't smoke?" I said, "Yes, that's true but don't worry about it. That's not important for you right now." And it wasn't important for him right then because he didn't have a testimony of the church

So we pushed that aside. When we got to the point where we had taught him about the gospel so that he had a testimony, we asked him the questions: Is Joseph Smith a true prophet? and is the church restored? He said "Yes".

Then we said, "Remember when we told you it wasn't important about your smoking? Well, NOW it is important!"

Now, living the gospel is important! After they have a testimony of the church, the commandments become important. Before that, the commandments are not important to the investigators <u>because they are not going to change without a testimony</u>.

I have talked to investigators about not smoking, about not living with their girlfriend, early in the discussion and they have thought about that and they said to themselves, "Well, I'm not going to give up smoking. I could never quit smoking so there's no point in visiting with these Mormons any more. I don't need to hear what they say because I'm not going to change." I have lost many investigators before the importance of a testimony was revealed to me.

REASON TO QUIT SMOKING

I was praying about what to do and it came to me in revelation as surely as any revelation I have had in my life. People won't quit for themselves, or for their spouse. They certainly won't quit for the missionaries. <u>The only way people quit smoking successfully is to show their love for Jesus Christ</u>.

CHAPTER EIGHT

THE "COMMIT TO CHRIST TO QUIT SMOKING" DISCUSSION

One of the great problems that I had was when the investigator gets to the point where he has a testimony of the Church and is still smoking. They need to quit smoking to join the Church.

Smoking is a very powerful addiction. How many have had problems getting people to quit smoking? Most of the Elders and Sisters have raised their hands. I lost a lot of investigators before this was revealed to me. I was praying about what to do and it came to me in a revelation that most people won't quit for themselves, but they will for the Lord. It is up to you as representatives of the Lord to make that real for them.

President Christensen, (Pres. of Arkansas Little Rock Mission) would you come up here? President Christensen is our non-member. Can you visualize him as a non-member? Can you visualize Pres. Christensen with a cigarette? Never. O.K.

A COMMITMENT TO CHRIST

Now this is a commitment to Christ to stop smoking. We have been teaching Brother Christensen to the point where he has answered those key questions:

Was Joseph Smith a true prophet? Yes.

Is the Church of Jesus Christ of Latter-Day Saints the Lord's true church? Yes.

Now in the process of coming to that realization, we have had spiritual experiences together, as a missionary and an investigator, Brother Christensen loves me. The Spirit of the Lord has been with us in these discussions. Your investigators will love you when you reach that point of approaching baptism. Having that love and spirit there makes this discussion successful. This is the way it goes:

"Brother Christensen, do you have some young children?"

"Yes."

"You probably tell them not to play in the street. Is that true?"

"That's true."

"Why do you tell them not to play in the street?"

"Because I love them and I'm concerned about their welfare."

"You mean it's not because you don't want them to have fun?"

"Of course not."

"If your children played in the street against your wishes and got hurt - how would you feel?"

"Terrible."

"Why?"

"Because I love them and I'm concerned when anything happens to them."

"So when your children hurt themselves, it hurts you. Brother Christensen, can you see how that is like our Father in Heaven? He has told us not to do certain things. Not because He doesn't want us to have fun but because He loves us. He is our Father as you are your children's father. And He loves us the way you love your children, perhaps even more. Do you love your Father in Heaven?"

"Yes."

I know you do. As we taught you the gospel we have felt the Lord's love as we shared the gospel with you. Do you love the Saviour?

"Yes."

"We know you have a strong love for the Saviour. When you break the commandments the Lord has given you and hurt yourself, how do you think the Lord feels?"

"I'm sure he feels bad."

Do you understand that when you hurt yourself, you hurt the Lord?

Brother Christensen, do you want to hurt the Lord?

"No, I don't."

"I know you don't. Because you love the Lord you want to do everything you can to make Him proud of you and avoid hurting Him. Understanding that He has a great love for you, you want to do everything He has asked you to do because you know that He loves you. He has given you commandments out of love. Brother Christensen, I know we have had some wonderful experiences visiting and talking together. We talked about our love for the Savior, I want you to imagine what it would be like if the Savior, himself were to appear in this room in a brilliant light, standing above the floor and were to call you by name, how would you feel if that would happen?"

"I'd be overwhelmed."

"You would be overwhelmed."

"Brothers and sisters, at this point you pull out a picture of the Savior and hold it so Brother Christensen can focus on it to help him to visualize the love he has for the Savior. The Spirit will be very strong.

"Brother Christensen, as the Savior appears in the room and calls you by name, He tells you that He loves you and you express your love for him. Your feelings would be overwhelming. You would feel a tremendous love for the Savior, in fact, I feel it now, do you?"

"Yes."

IDENTIFY THE SPIRIT
You identify the spirit to Brother Christensen, bear your testimony of the Savior and testify that the spirit

and feelings that he is having are the Spirit of the Lord testifying to the truth.

"Brother Christensen, if the Lord asked you to do something to show your love for him, what would you say to Him as you stand before Him?"

"Yes."

"Why would you say yes?"

"Because of my love and respect for Him".

"I know that is true, Brother Christensen. The Lord has sent us here today as representatives of Him, representatives of Jesus Christ, to ask if you love Him enough to give up smoking for 24 hours. Brother Christensen, do you love Him enough to give up smoking for Him, to keep His commandments so you won't hurt yourself and thereby hurt Him?"

"Yes, I do."

"I know you do."

"Brothers and Sisters, because of the love the investigator has for the Savior, he will keep that commandment and because it is a small commitment he will keep it for 24 hours. He can do it for 24 hours. Brothers and Sisters, we are going to come back within 24 hours to see if he still loves the Savior enough tomorrow to promise another 24 hours. I promise you he will."

A SEVEN DAY COMMITMENT

"Brother Christensen, we are going to do this for seven days, on the seventh day you are going to show your ultimate love to the Savior by taking upon yourself His name and follow His Commandment for all his children to be baptized in His Church by the proper authority. How do you feel about that, Brother Christensen?"

"That sounds wonderful. I know it won't be easy but I know it is possible and I know if I keep those commandments, I will be blessed."

"You will be blessed, Brother Christensen." Brothers and Sisters this is one of the keys. You will virtually live with Brother Christensen for the next week. You will call him on the phone and you will <u>absolutely visit him every 24 hours</u> and re-commit him. You will talk to him constantly about his love for the Savior, giving him a spiritual experience every day for seven days. On the seventh day he will be baptized and it will be a glorious experience for him, and for you too!

BEGINNING WITH DAY ONE

The first day you will leave him a picture of the Savior.

The next day you might come back and leave him a white rose to signify his pure love for the Savior and how pure he will be when he is baptized.

The following day you might bring appropriate scriptures to read. Each day you must bring something. You must not miss. You must be there before the 24 hours are up or he may have a cigarette in one hand and a lighter in the other, watching the clock.

This will work. All the times I have presented this discussion, with the spirit, under the circumstances I have told you, no one has ever failed to quit smoking or to be baptized.

I have had many wonderful experiences with it. One that was particularly meaningful to me was a young man named Eric Larsen. He was in St. Louis in the Ward where I served.

I challenged him to go on a mission about fifty times. Finally I followed a hunch and bore testimony to him on the sidewalk outside the church. It was a very spiritual experience and he accepted that commitment to go on a mission.

He was sent to Taiwan on his mission. Taiwan was a tough mission. If you think this mission is tough, in Taiwan the average baptisms per missionary per year was less than one. There are missionaries that go the whole two years with NO baptisms! So it was a very tough mission.

When he had been on his mission some months, I heard that he was having a hard time and was getting discouraged. I was busy with my things, and didn't have time, but I had a hunch that I needed to send him a tape so I got out my tape recorder one "P" day and started making a tape. I had a hunch that I ought to send him this discussion on tape, "Commit to Christ to quit smoking!"

I said, "You know, Elder Larsen, I don't know why I'm sending this to you. I don't even know if people smoke in China. But nonetheless, I feel inspired to send it." So I recorded on the audio-cassette, the "Commit to Christ" discussion. Would it surprise you if I told you that on the other side of the world at that moment, we found out later, that Elder Larsen and his companion were having a great struggle with teaching an investigator, Mr. Wong.

They had committed him to be baptized. He believed that the church was true. He had gone to the font twice dressed in white but he couldn't be baptized because he hadn't quit smoking. What a disappointment! He hadn't had any baptisms. Here was his chance to have "the baptism of his mission" and his investigator hadn't quit smoking. Elder Larsen and his companion had prayed and fasted that the Lord would tell them what to do.

At that very time, we later learned, on the other side of the world in St. Louis, Missouri, I felt a hunch that I should send him this discussion. So I mailed it off and it got to him a week later. When he began to listen to the tape, the Spirit bore witness to him that it was a direct answer to his prayer.

He and his companion listened to the tape and practiced and practiced in their apartment how they would give this discussion to Mr. Wong.

Then they went over to Mr. Wong with a picture of the Savior and began giving this discussion. The Spirit was there! As they reached the point where they asked him to give up smoking to show his love for the Saviour, Mr. Wong began to tremble. Elder Larsen said, "I know it will be hard." Tears rolled down Mr. Wong's cheeks and he reached into his pocket and grabbed his cigarettes, pulled them out, tore them in two, threw them on the ground and stamped on them. Crying, he said, "Nothing is too hard for the Lord."

For the first time on his mission, Elder Larsen was able to stand in the waters of baptism and baptize Mr. Wong. Perhaps what is even more beautiful about this story, is that because of the great spirit of that baptism and the change in Mr. Wong, his entire family was baptized.

Brothers and Sisters, the Lord does use you and me to accomplish His miracles. He uses imperfect humans to do his work. Don't ask me why. I'm not really sure.

He could have given the same inspiration to Elder Larsen but for some reason He chose to do it this way. So always follow your hunches, follow the Spirit and you will have great spiritual experiences.

P.S.

I have been asked about other "Stop smoking" programs. I think they are wonderful! But use them after this "Commit to Christ to Stop Smoking "discussion." Merge the two together, but remember the more spiritual the presentation is, the more successful it will be.

CHAPTER NINE

PROBLEM: PEOPLE WHO WON'T READ
ANSWER: THE BOOK OF MORMON ON TRIAL

Next - one of the great problems that I had in teaching people and getting them ready for baptism is "investigators who won't read!" Does anybody have the problem of investigators who won't read? Well, I did and it seems most of you have too. What do you do with investigators who won't read? Do you take them a Book of Mormon or what?

You say, "Would you read these pages in the Book of Mormon?" and they won't read. What do you do? Read with them? That's one solution.

Brothers and sisters, they have to have a testimony that Joseph Smith is a true prophet, or to say it better - that Jesus Christ used Joseph Smith as an instrument in restoring the Church. I struggled with this. Are people who will not read not worthy to join the Church? Does the Lord want someone who can't read or won't read, not to join the Church? We have an obligation to the investigators for them to have every opportunity to get a testimony to join the Church. Just because they won't read, they should not be excluded from being a member of the Church and having those joys.

BOOK OF MORMON ON TRIAL

I found a great aid! It is called "The Book of Mormon on Trial." Have you ever seen or read this book? Only one person out of the group has. Let me tell you what it is. "The Book of Mormon on Trial" is a cartoon version of a true event that occurred to Jack West.

It is available at www.BookofMormonTrial.com

Have any of you heard of Jack West? Jack West was studying law and for his final thesis he decided that he would defend the Book of Mormon as being the Word of God in a court of law, in a mock trial. His instructor was the "judge" and all the other students in the class were the opposition, the prosecuting attorneys. Jack West stood as defense to defend the Book of Mormon as the Word of God and a true book of scripture and that Joseph Smith was a Prophet.

A MOCK TRIAL

In this "Mock Trial" they went through three main areas concerning the Book of Mormon.

#1 Witnesses who knew Joseph Smith, who saw the Book of Mormon, and handled it and what happened to them the rest of their lives.

#2 Internal evidences of the Book of Mormon relating to the Bible and other scriptures and writings.

#3 Archaeological evidences of the Book of Mormon.

Three sections in the trial. At the conclusion of the trial of the Book of Mormon, Jack West proved in the Court that the Book of Mormon was the Word of God, on all counts. It's a great story. It has been compiled into this cartoon version and also in a printed version. As I said this is for investigators who cannot or will not read. This book will help them to have a testimony of the Church.

In teaching out of this book, first we would try to see if they would read it on their own. I remember one occasion we gave this to the family and the 11 year old daughter read 2/3 of the Book of Mormon on Trial the first night and already had a testimony of the gospel before the rest of the family did. How hard is it to get an 11 year old to have a testimony that Joseph Smith is a true prophet? It's not easy.

But for the investigators who read it, the Spirit testifies strongly to them. Sometimes I would give it to more educated people and say, "Listen, I know you are a busy person and you have a lot of demands on your time. I have a pamphlet here in cartoon form that you can skim and read in an hour and a half. Would you mind doing that, I don't want to offend you."

When I first started using this I had people on rare occasions say, "Do you think I'm a kid? That I can't read?" But when I presented it in a humble way, they didn't feel that way and even very intellectual people found this to be an interesting book. We also used these as lesson manuals to share the gospel.

We would have one for each investigator. You need three or four of them. It's a good idea to get a cover on them because using them as much as we did they become rather ragged. We targeted certain pages and rather than read every page in there, we would start out with page 72 which is the story of Joseph Smith. It talks about the First Vision, things that happened to Joseph Smith, then we would skip ahead and start into the Three Witnesses.

THREE WITNESSES VIDEO

Do you know that the Three Witnesses video is a marvelous tool the Lord has given us to prove that the Church is true? How many have seen the video of the Three Witnesses? Everyone should see that. Everyone. It is an important tool to help people know that the Church is true. As Jack West points out in "Book of Mormon on Trial," one of the primary ways that we know something is true is by the testimony of the people who were there.

You ask someone, "Why do you believe the Bible is true?" The bottom line is, it's because most people believe that Matthew, Mark, Luke and John were telling the truth. They believe that Matthew, Mark, Luke and John were true witnesses of the Lord and the things he did. Oliver Cowdery, David Whitmer, and Martin Harris were true witnesses of the Book of Mormon. By concentrating on their experiences, we can build a powerful case that proves their honesty to our investigator. It gives them intellectual, and hopefully, spiritual knowledge that they were telling the truth.

WHY DID THEY LEAVE?

One of the parts we like to read is on page 122, - Oliver Cowdery was a lawyer and as you may know, all three of the witnesses were excommunicated or otherwise left the Church. Your investigators will say, "Well, why would they leave the Church? Why did they get kicked out if they had a testimony?"

The answer is: "Because they became swelled up in pride in their hearts. They thought that since they were so important, that they had seen the Angel and had handled the Gold Plates that they should be entitled to important positions in the Church. They also thought they should be apostles and have a hand in the direction of the Church.

The Lord didn't see it that way and when He didn't, they became bitter toward Joseph Smith. This makes their testimony even more powerful. Even though they were excommunicated from the Church and personally disaffected with Joseph Smith, they held true to their testimony.

One time when Oliver Cowdery was defending a case in court, the opposing attorney said, "How can you believe anything this man says? A man, who in the front of the Book of Mormon, claims that he saw an angel."

Oliver stood up and said, "May it please the Court and Gentlemen of the Jury: My brother attorney on the other side has charged me with the connection of Joseph Smith and the 'Golden Bible'." (Keep in mind that he had been out of the church many years at this point and as we said was disaffected by Joseph Smith).

"The responsibility has been placed upon me and I cannot escape reply. Before God and man, <u>I dare not deny</u> what I have said - what my testimony contains, as written and printed on the first page of the Book of Mormon. May it please your Honor and gentlemen of the jury, this I say: <u>I saw the angel</u> and heard the voice from Heaven. How can I deny it?"

"It happened in the daytime when the sun was shin-

67

ing brightly in the firmament, not at night when I was asleep. The glorious messenger from heaven, dressed in a white robe, standing above the ground in a glory I have never seen anything to compare with, the sun insignificant in comparison, told us if we denied that testimony there is no forgiveness in this life or in the world to come. <u>How can I deny it</u>? <u>I dare not, I will not</u>."

This is in the court record, brothers and sisters. This is not just recorded by Mormon writers somewhere. This is history. Oliver Cowdrey held true to his beliefs his entire life as did the other three witnesses. As he said, this happened in the daytime, this wasn't at night when he was asleep. <u>It was outside</u>! A powerful experience! If you had an experience like that, wouldn't you testify to it all your life? These men lived more than 40 years after Joseph Smith was dead. These are the things I would be saying to my investigators:

What are the odds that someone would continue to testify of these things if they were not true? It is interesting, even in anti-Mormon literature, that they admit that these three witnesses held true to their testimony.

ANTI-MORMON LITERATURE

Pres. Christensen said earlier that you have been exposed to anti-Mormon literature, too. Well, we were exposed to plenty of it. All of our people who were baptized had anti-Mormon literature given to them by friends and ministers. It is a fact of life in the mission field, you cannot avoid it.

I concluded that I would inoculate investigators the best I could by getting to them first. I copied a page of rather innocent, not really sophisticated, anti-Mormon literature to show them that some people were against the Church unreasonably. I then explained that prejudiced people told lies and biased facts about the Church. I then helped them understand just how strong the testimony of the three witnesses is.

Here is a sample of anti-Mormon literature: On one page it says that "on January 18th of that year Joseph eloped with his landlord's daughter, Emma Hale, and married her against her parents will." (How shocking!)

But here's the good part:

"One day in 1829, Joseph Smith took these three men into the woods to show them the golden plates. After spending a long time in prayer, they saw the sacred documents in a vision. They recorded their vision in writing and this signed testimony is in the front of every copy of the Book of Mormon. They always stood by their statement though they were expelled by the Mormons in 1838 after a quarrel with Joseph Smith.

Martin Harris lived to the age of 92. With his last words he testified to the truth of the vision. On his death bed, Oliver Cowdrey said to David Whitmer, "Brother David, remain true to your testimony about the Book of Mormon."

David Whitmer even had engraved on his tombstone, "The Charter of the Jews, i.e. (the Old Testament), and the Charter of the Nephites, (the Book of Mormon) are One Truth Eternal." The honesty of these three men cannot be doubted. Whether Joseph Smith put them into a state of collective hypnosis or deceived them with some homemade plates, cannot be known for certain. "(I have to wonder if the author of this anti-Mormon literature noticed how unlikely this would be!)"

Brothers and Sisters, the Church is true! It really is! As you share this truth with your investigators, they will also know it is true. I have never used The "Book of Mormon on Trial" and taught all the way through it and not had an investigator have the intellectual testimony of the Church. Then when we would ask the investigator:

"Is Joseph Smith a true prophet?

"Yes, he is."

"Is the Church of Jesus Christ of Latter Day Saints the True Church?"

"Yes, it is."

I cannot ever remember teaching all the way through this book without getting the correct answers to those questions.

Now, we did not baptize everyone that said yes because some of those people had only an intellectual belief that the church was true. You have to have a spiritual belief also.

"The Book of Mormon on Trial" is just one of many tools that you can use to help your investigators.

Hopefully, all of you will have multiple discussions that you can teach your investigators, so before you walk in the door, you can pray about what you are going to teach them. You need to have a repertoire of discussions and have a choice of different things to choose. I would recommend that you have access to 'The Three Witnesses' and use that as one of your early discussions to help people to have a testimony of the Book of Mormon.

THE PERSISTENT "BORN AGAIN"

The Book of Mormon is a valuable tool the Lord has given us. Use it to it's maximum benefit. There is opposition to the Church. I remember one time there was a "Born Again" who wanted to 'save' us missionaries. He was very persistent. He came over to our apartment. He wanted to visit and teach us so we said, "We want to teach you." I thought if we have him over here at 9:00 a.m. we can get the first discussion in before we leave the apartment!

So we invited him over. As I said, using your time effectively is so important and the morning and afternoon hours are low in value. So when we could schedule and teach discussions in the morning and use those hours to their highest use, which is teaching, that is a great use of the Lord's time.

You are out on your mission for just a flash. You will be home before you know it and you will be looking back. There will come a day, if you have worked hard and served your mission as you should, that you would give anything if you could relive just one day of your mission. So use your mission time wisely.

CHAPTER TEN

THE UNBEATABLE POSITION DISCUSSION

So we invited this guy over and he talked about all the things the 'born-agains' like to talk about regarding the Church. We weren't getting anywhere so I finally stopped him and said, "O.K. Mr. Smith, let me ask you this."

(We call this the unbeatable position in the course.) Mr. Smith, what does it take to be Saved in the Kingdom of God? What does it take to go to Heaven? Mr. Smith, in your belief, what does it take?

He said, "Well, you have to accept Jesus Christ as your Saviour."

I said, "O.K. What else does it take? Do you have to be baptized?"

He said, "Well, No. Baptism is just an outward sign of your inward change. You don't have to be baptized."

Now, some people will say that you have to be baptized, so I would say, "Baptized by whom?" And in most religions they will say "You have to be baptized by a "believer in Christ"". This is true in virtually all religions.

"So do you need to do any good works?"

"Oh, no. It is by grace that you are saved - not by works."

Now we need to repeat it back to him.

So I'd say, "Now let me get this straight - in order to be saved I have to accept Jesus Christ as my Saviour and nothing else. Does this mean - once saved - always saved?" He said Yes! (It's surprising how many believe that. So I said, "Mr. Smith, I've got some great news for you. By your standards - Mormons are going to Heaven!"

He asked, "What do you mean?"

I said, "Well, all Mormons believe that before they can become a member of the Church, they have to accept Jesus Christ as their Saviour. And furthermore, every Mormon has been baptized by a believer in Christ. Every priesthood holder believes in Christ. So every member of the Church has been baptized by a person who believes in Christ. Furthermore Mormons also believe that they should keep the commandments to show their love for Christ.

He said, "Well, we don't believe that - By grace you are saved, not by works."

"O.K., then what you are saying is that Mormons are trying too hard to be saved."

He said, "But Joseph Smith was a false prophet!"

I said, "So? I testify to you that Joseph Smith was a True Prophet, but even if he were a false prophet - by your standard I'm going to Heaven! Right?"

"But, but, but..." He was speechless. He was absolutely speechless!

You should share this with your investigators. When

their friends are telling them that Mormons are wrong, and they are getting anti-Mormon literature, they need the reassurance. Brothers and Sisters, we have that reassurance.

<u>We have all the good</u> things that can be found <u>in any other church, plus more!</u> You present this to your investigator, that by the standards of their former church that they will go to Heaven.

There is no draw-back in becoming a member of the Church. It knocks down one more obstacle on the road to baptism.

Now, on rare occasions, and of course this usually wouldn't happen with your investigator, but if you are dealing with a minister of another religion, someone well-read in anti-Mormon literature, they might say, "Well, yeah, but you Mormons believe in a different Jesus Christ than is in the Bible."

To that I would say, "You mean that the Jesus Christ we believe in is a separate, distinct being from His Father? So what you're really talking about is that our concept of Jesus Christ's body is different from your concept of Jesus Christ's body".

THE TRINITY CREATION

They believe in the trinity creation. The trinity was voted on in the Council of Nicene hundreds of years after Christ's death. A bunch of church leaders and government officials got together and voted on "who God was?", and it wasn't even a unanimous vote.

There were about four different versions of God that

were voted on. The version that is used by Catholics and Protestants today only won by about a 40 percent margin. Their view of God, as you may know, is that He is like a formless mass of spirit that fills the whole universe and when He comes to earth, part of it breaks off and forms itself into Jesus.

"So what you are talking about is that our understanding of God's body is different than yours. Are you saying that to be "saved" you have to understand what God's body is made of and that having faith in Jesus Christ as your Saviour is not enough unless you understand what his body is made of?"

"Well uh, No."

"So by faith you are saved, not by understanding what Christ's body is made of." (John 3:16 to 3:18 makes this perfectly clear.)

"Well, right."

"If your God, the Christ that you worship, would keep His children out of the Kingdom of Heaven because they didn't know what His body was made of, maybe we do worship a different Jesus Christ."

That sums it up. Right?

BIBLE BASHING

I'm not trying to teach you to 'bash' or maybe I am. Let me just say this about 'Bible bashing'. Don't do it. Don't ever compare scriptures with people who are against the Church. When I walk into a discussion and

75

there is a minister and his aids sitting on one side of the table, my investigators sitting in the middle and they want me to sit on the other side, my scriptures would never get unzipped.

I would just sit down and I would testify and bear witness to the truth of the Church and talk about the Book of Mormon and our unbeatable position. I would never argue the scriptures. Arguing the scriptures gets you nowhere, creates tension and I don't know that I was good enough to do it anyway. But I never had to back down when I presented, with the Spirit, things that I've told you about our unbeatable position, and the things in the "Where Can I Find Something Better" chapter.

Another thing - I do have one scripture that I really enjoy. We had an investigator, a young girl, who was going to be baptized. Her minister came over and told her how 'the Mormons were bad, she was going to go to Hell', and all these other things. He gave her all this anti-Mormon literature. She called us up in tears. We went over and talked to her and she started presenting all these things, she was crying and she was upset.

II TIMOTHY

I remembered a scripture in II Timothy that my Mission President had taught us so I opened up the scriptures to II Timothy, 1st chapter, verse 7, and after she had told, in her tears, the terrible things the Church was accused of, we read this to her:

"For God has not given us the spirit of fear, but of power and of love and of a sound mind." (II Timothy 1:7) I said to her: "Laurie, as we have taught you the gospel of Jesus Christ, what sort of a spirit have you felt in our discussions?"

She brightened up, looked at me and said, "I felt the Spirit of power and of love and of sound mind."

"When your minister came to you and was teaching you things he had to say about the Mormons, what did you feel?"

She said, "I felt the spirit of fear and darkness."

"What does that tell you?"

She smiled.

She was baptized three days later.

What does that tell you?

CHAPTER ELEVEN

GOING HOME

When I came out on my mission, the first day I came into the Mission Home, there were some Elders going home. They had long hair and they were laughing and joking. They were kind of a rowdy bunch, and I was surprised because I had just come from the MTC. I was all pumped up and these Elders were so glad to be going home. One came up to me and said, "Elder, if I had as long to go on my mission as you do, I would slash my wrists." Then he laughed.

I was shocked! I had given up so much to go on my mission and here was an Elder making fun of the fact that I was just starting and he was finishing.

I had companions who would, on the last week of their mission, ceremoniously burn a white shirt every day the last seven days of their mission. "Well, there's another one I'll never wear again!" I hope none of you know of anyone who's ever done that.

I had companions who couldn't wait to go home. One would sit on his bed and draw pictures of airplanes and suitcases at night. I'll tell you what - we were both counting days until he went home. I know <u>I was marking my calendar</u>!

I made a promise to myself and the Lord that that would never happen to me, that I would work with all my heart, might, mind and strength every day of my mission. The thing that I'm most proud of from my mission is not that I held the record for the number of baptisms and several other records because those things were gifts from God. <u>The thing that I'm most proud of is that I worked hard my whole mission. The baptisms were gifts from God that He gave to me. My work was my gift to Him. Each of you can do that. There were missionaries just as good and just as spiritual as I was, who had very few baptisms. And you should know that it is true that the number of baptisms does not necessarily indicate the power of the missionary.</u>

Certainly we need to strive with all our heart. Don't use excuses. Don't say "Oh, this is a real hard area, the members aren't any good, nobody ever baptizes in this area." <u>Don't believe it! Those five people are there for you to baptize and you can do it.</u>

I promised that I would go tracting on the last day of my mission. I made that goal that I would work up to the very last day and I would put all thoughts of my fiancee, girls, Corvette's, and everything else out of my mind until after my mission.

My fiancee wrote to me every day for a year and a half, but of course you know that a mission is two years long. So I finally got that famous "Dear John" letter - which I still have, by the way, but things worked out. The Lord blesses those who serve Him and are willing to "Lock their hearts" during their missions.

I extended my mission one month so that I could go around and talk to the missionaries. I gave 23 of these seminars the last month of my mission. At the end of 30 days I was exhausted but it was wonderful! Because I was late going home, I was the only missionary left so the Mission President called me and said, "Elder Marshall, I was going to meet you tomorrow before you go to the airport but something has come up. I have an appointment at Springfield, which is about 3 hours from the mission home, I need you to come to the office tomorrow morning at 7:00 o'clock and ride up with me to Springfield. I can just barely get you back to the airport in time to put you on the plane." I really wanted to talk to the Mission President so I said "O.K".

As I hung up I thought, "Oh boy, I promised myself and the Lord that I would tract on the last day of my mission. How am I going to keep that promise now?" Next day I went down to the mission office and President and I rode up to Springfield. We had a great visit on the way. When we got there, he did something that I had never known to happen before, he got out of the car, tossed me the keys and said, "Here, Elder, go get yourself something to eat. Come back in an hour."

I was turned loose with the Mission President's car all by myself! One missionary in a lone and dreary world. As I drove away in the president's car I thought, "Here's my chance to go tracting, but I need somebody to tract with!" Having traveled in the mission I knew where the missionaries apartment was, it was about noon, so I went over there. I pulled in front of the apartment. Coincidentally, there were two sets of Elders there having lunch. Were they every surprised! "Elder Marshall, what are you doing here? You are supposed to go home today." I said, "Yes, but I have to do some tracting first."

They looked at me like I was crazy, which was nothing new. I said, "I need one of you Elders to come with me right now." We only had about 30 minutes so I said, "We can't go far. Has this street been tracted?"

They looked at each other and said, "I don't know." So I said, "O.K. we'll do this street." We walked right out of the missionaries door, crossed the street and knocked on the door. We were invited in. We taught a great discussion, placed a Book of Mormon with the people and made a return appointment.

I like to loan a "Book of Mormon" rather than give them away. We sold Book of Mormons when I was on my mission but I like to loan it instead. It gave us a return appointment because we were going to come back and pick up our book! We might come back to pick it up and say, "Well, you can have it as a gift from us." Anyway, we made that appointment for the other Elders to return, and walked out the door.

There were only 10 minutes left before I had to go back. We walked to the next door which was also right across from the missionaries apartment. Missionaries had been in that apartment probably 10 to 20 years.

We knocked on the door and an older lady answered the door. We asked, "may we come in for just a moment. We can't stay but we have an exciting message from Jesus Christ." We made a return appointment, talked about the Gospel and were out of there in about 10 minutes. I went back across the street, jumped in the car, drove down and picked up the President. We went back to St. Louis, I got on the plane and flew home.

An interesting thing - the lady who lived behind that last door, which was right across the street from those missionaries, joined the Church a month later. A year later, the lady went on a mission. How many lives were touched? What if I had not gone tracting that last day of my mission?

YOU CAN MAKE DEALS

Brothers and Sisters, you can make deals with the Lord. And do you know what? He keeps his end. You promise the Lord that you will do what's right, and He will bless you beyond your imagination.

On the way home on the airplane, I thought about what I was going to do with the rest of my life. And do you know what - before the plane landed in Salt Lake, I had my whole life planned out!

While on my mission, <u>I didn't need to think about what I was going to do when I got home</u>. There's lots of time to think about that while you're on the plane.

Brothers and Sisters, work hard, put all thoughts of home, girl friends, boy friends, everything out of your mind and serve the Lord your whole mission with all your heart, might, mind and strength. <u>After all - that's what you promised you would do!</u>

The End.

CHAPTER TWELVE

WHERE CAN I FIND SOMETHING BETTER?
   This is a post I put on Face Book.

Hey Gang,
   I love to learn about other religions, and I never have unpleasant experiences talking to people about their beliefs. It's pretty fun.
   Here's what I have learned.

   Some of the first questions I have about a faith are:
   1. What is your source of truth? Most religions will hold up an ancient Book, usually the Koran, the Bible, the Torah, etc.
   2. What makes your reading of this ancient Book, the correct understanding of the original Author? (I am amazed that so many will claim that their interpretation of is the ONLY possible meaning to a verse)

   They always agree that nothing is more important than knowing the truth about who God is, and who you are to him, but, people devote hardly any time to finding the most truth about God. I have. After all, "There is no advantage in believing something about God that is not true."

   All religions claim to have the most truth about God, as well they should. Why be in a religion that claims to be the second most true?
   I always focus on the <u>positive</u> in my investigations. I want to learn how my life would be better if my family was a part of their faith.

   I want the best for my family. Why settle for second best?

So I say,-- Tell me the good things in your faith. What does it take to be saved? How does one lose their salvation?

I noticed a pattern in my investigation, All faiths, Christian and otherwise, would like their members to do the same things, (in essence, live the 10 commandments) but, they have different success rates at doing so.

Getting results are important.

So I wrote an article about a year ago. I have given out hundreds of these but have had no luck yet.

Does anybody have a better answer? Here it is.

Where Can I Find Something Better?

I was raised in a protestant faith until Mormon missionaries found me and baptized me as a young man. I have continued to study other faiths for over thirty years and I have been amazed at all the anti-Mormon materials in print, film and on the internet. I am an inquisitive and practical soul, so I have searched out the answers to the multitude of "problems" critics of the Mormon faith have claimed. After considering both sides, I cannot break loose of the Church's hold on me because of the following reasons:

(1) The Mormon Church has instilled in me, and my family a more deep and personal love of my Savior Jesus Christ than I could have reached in any other faith. I have a sure knowledge that He is my Savior and the only One through whom I can be saved. The Book of Mormon has added so much to the wonderful accounts of Him in the New Testament. The testimony and lives of good Mormons have led me to know that they are true followers of Christ. While I have met wonderful Christians in other faiths, none have stronger belief in the Savior than good Mormons. Help me! Where can I find something better?

(2) The Mormons taught me that I am a child of God created in His image, and not just His creation. (Genesis 1:26 "And God said Let us make man in our image, after our likeness" The Trinity is The Father, The Son, and The Holy Ghost. Three separate Beings with one purpose. The other faiths taught me that God is one Being with three names, The Father, The Son, and The Holy Ghost. And that He is a Spirit without form that fills the whole universe. While this sounds impressive, it would mean that He is only my Creator and not my Father in Heaven. I would be just one of His creations. For example, I can create a beautiful Corvette, and I would love it, but it can never compare with the love I have for my children. I know that my Father in Heaven <u>is my Father</u> in Heaven-and that is much more intimate and personal for me, than to love a Father who is an intangible Spirit - Creator, to whom I am just something He created. The net result is that my children and I have a much more personal relationship with God, and His Son, Jesus Christ. Where can I find something better?

(3) Eternal Marriage and families - What an awesome demonstration of the love and Fatherhood of God. Mormons are the only faith that believes that God ordained the family as an Eternal unit. All other faiths teach that marriage ends at death. Because of this belief, Mormon families are the strongest (on average) of any people on Earth. I know from personal experience, that these teachings have helped me and my children to have stronger families in Christ. Where can I find something better?

(4) The Church missionary system: The Mormon church offers a chance for my children to voluntarily serve as full time representatives of the Lord for two years. Every Christian religion says it believes Christ's admonition to "feed My sheep" and share His Word, but, none, not even

the Jehovah's Witnesses have as good a means to make it a positive and life changing experience as the Mormons. I did this myself, and I know from personal experience that nothing can replace the experience, joy and testimony of Jesus Christ I received on my two year mission. I now know why the Bible emphasizes sharing His Word so much. Why do other faiths not promote programs like this for their members? Some offer "mission trips" lasting days or weeks, but this is only a pale shadow of the Mormons two year program. Some faiths have full time missionaries, but their numbers are so small compared to their membership, and they don't encourage all their youth to go on missions. As many as half of Mormon youth go on missions. I have often said that it is worth being a Mormon just for the blessing of seeing my children have the two year mission experience when they are young. Where can I find something better?

(5) The Mormon Health Code - Why don't other faiths do this? I need help teaching my children to avoid alcohol, tobacco and drugs. All faiths believe the body is a temple, but none have as much success teaching their children to avoid unhealthy habits, as do the Mormons. It would be worth being a Mormon just to avoid the problems of seeing my children and grandchildren suffer from the effects of alcohol and drugs, not to mention tobacco. Where can I find something better?

(6) Unpaid Ministry - Mormons don't have to get paid to share the good news of Jesus Christ. I have always had a problem with ministers who would say, "Give your money to God, but make the check out to me." Mormon leaders of congregations (called bishops) have regular jobs. That is how they support themselves and they serve the congregation for free because they love the Lord. Mormons actually provide better support to each member of the congregation than faiths with paid preachers, because of the organization

of visiting and home teachers, (also unpaid) that help the bishops check the welfare of every member every month! No other faith comes close to that service for the members, even with paid ministry. Even the two-year missionaries pay their own way. It works great. There is no reason other faiths could not do this too. Why don't they?

I love knowing that when I come to church, that they are glad to see me because they care about me and not about what donations I might give them. Also, Mormons don't have collection plates. Giving is personal and private and visitors are treated like guests. You would not invite a friend to dinner and then put a collection plate in his face and say "Wasn't that good?" Also, I have investigated the way the Church uses funds and it is inspiring. Where can I find something better?

On top of all this, while opponents fuss that false prophets lead us, the Bible clearly states repeatedly that it is through the Name of Jesus that we are saved. Virtually all other Christians believe that if we accept Christ as our Savior we are saved. By this standard, all Mormons are saved, even if we did have "false" prophets. I must say that if we are to judge prophets by their fruits, then I am really caught by the Mormons, because of all the wonderful "fruits" I have personally witnessed over the last thirty years. I could go on and on, but, the bottom line is that because of all the blessings and happiness I have received, I guess I am going to have to stay with the Mormons. Please help me if you know anything that is better.

Scott Marshall
2282 Whitten Rd. Memphis, TN. 38133
901-372-7421 cell
www.MemphisBPC@AOL.com

Now the key aspects of this missionary tool are:

- #1 Testifies of our strong testimony of the Savior to dispel the belief we are not "saved".
- #2 Many people believe this even though their church does not, and it reemphasizes our personal relationship with Christ to be saved.
- #3 Strong families are sought by all.
- #4 This opens up opportunity to talk about temples and how much they love their families.
- #5 Others believe this too, but we <u>get</u> results, and that matters a lot.
- #6 Unpaid ministry is appreciated by all.

Again, it is important to testify of Christ, (as in #1 and #2) <u>first</u> in all you do, to add power to it, and dispel the ridiculous accusation that we are not Christians.

The way to distribute this, is to get the members to carry a condensed single folded page in their wallet. You never know when you will have a missionary moment and you need to give something with your contact information and testimony on the spot. Your wallet is always with you. When I give one out, I put another one back in my wallet when I get home. I urge the members to plagiarize and copy this into their personal testimony. The central article will fit on one 8 ½ by 11 page with small font. It is important to keep it one page so people will read it. When I give it out, I refer to it as "an article I wrote" rather than "my testimony" because non-members may misunderstand the meaning of "testimony".

I have given out hundreds of these and have never had anything but positive comments, even from ministers. I can e-mail you a copy of this that is formatted to fit on one page if you contract me at <u>MemphisBPC@aol.com</u>.

SUMMARY PAGES

TRACTING AND INSPIRATION
<u>Selecting areas to tract:</u>

1. Each missionary prays individually 5 to 15 min.
2. Combined prayer seeking inspiration.
3. First Elder reads off 5 to 15 streets off map following hunches. (inspiration)
4. Second Elder writes down street names the first Elder is reading out on piece of paper.
5. Both Elders seek for inspiration as they individually select 5 streets that look particularly good.
6. Compare separate lists to see which streets coincide.
7. Go tract the streets that coincide with a Positive Mental Attitude!
8. Do not doubt your inspiration for the Lord will bless you for the faith that you have exercised.

TRACTING:
1. When approaching the door
   a. Look toward the window
   b. Knock as you stand close to the door. Step back when non-member opens first door. Body language indicates you expect them to open second door and invite you in.
   c. Look people in the eye. The spirit is conveyed through the eyes.
   d. Smile and look pleasant. Say: Hi, how are you?

2. Identify who you are; and ask a question.
   a. We're representatives of the Church of Jesus Christ of Latter Day Saints, have you ever known any Mormons before?

b. I'm Elder Marshall and this is Elder Kilgore, we're ministers with the Church of Jesus Christ Latter Day Saints, have you ever known any Mormons before? (If they answer no ask: Have you ever heard of the Mormon Church?)

3. Actual approach.
   a. We're sharing a really exciting message today, could we visit with you for a few minutes?
   b. We're helping people to have a better understanding of the Mormons by telling them a little bit about how the church got started and some of our basic beliefs, may we visit with you?
   c. We're looking for people, who would be interested in learning more about the Mormon Church, would you be interested?

4. Objections and response.
   a. We have our own church.
      Answer: We understand that you have your own church, would you be interested for your own information to learn a little bit about the Mormons?
   b. We're really busy right now. (too busy / no time)
      Answer: Could we come back at another time and visit with you?
   c. I know all about the Mormons!
      Answer: We have something really exciting to share with you that I'm sure you haven't heard before and I'm positive you'll find it interesting, may we visit with you?

Get two rejections before leaving.
If the spirit directs that they are not going to be interested simply say have a good day!

ORGANIZATION AND TIME USAGE

Ask yourself every hour, "What is the highest use for this next hour?" while looking in your planner.

Always get name and phone number of tracting call backs and call them, to confirm visits.
When making appointments, always give two choices, (would tonight or tomorrow be better?)

Try to fill 8:30pm appointments first.
Recognize that 6:00 to 9:30pm and all day Saturday and Sunday are of highest value for missionary work. Spend these hours contacting non-members. Members can many times be contacted 8:30am to 6:00pm or when 8:30pm appointments fail.

Church meetings are the best place to do member missionary work. Split up and talk to as many different members as possible, if you do not have investigators present.

Much missionary time is lost traveling!!!! Do not drive or travel anywhere without asking yourself:
1. Can this trip be made later at a more efficient time?
2. Can this trip be done over the phone?
3. Can someone else better solve this need for a trip?
4. Can we combine this trip with later trips?
5. Is it better to just mail it in?
6. Call to confirm (a) Are they going to be there? (b) You know how to get there. (get directions) (c) Is the store, etc, open? (d) Are you bringing everything you need?
7. Use a checklist to insure you don't forget something!

INVITING PEOPLE TO CHURCH

- Invite to "Pre-visit" Church
- Invite on Saturday night for Sunday
- Confirm invitation on Sunday two hours before services
- Greet visitors before they get to the door of the Church
- Give visitors tour of the facilities
- Have companion "Birddog" members
- Sit visitors up front

A missionary or properly instructed fellowshipping member will be with visitor at all times to help them feel comfortable. This is especially important for young children and all youth.

If there are no visitors:

Stay where you can spot late visitors preferably where you can view the congregation and the parking lot.

If you are new in a ward find a knowledgeable member and ask them to help you identify and memorize members and non- members.

Ask everyone if they know anyone to invite to Church Split up and sit with different families each week to get to know them better.

Ask the Bishop if missionaries may speak for 2 minutes after announcements each sacrament meeting to make members more aware of the missionaries.

OUTLINE OF COMMIT TO CHRIST

1. Have a spiritually receptive setting, quiet and uninterrupted.

2. Talk of a parent's love for their children.

3. Talk of a parent's rules of love - commandments.

4. Talk of a parent's pain when children hurt themselves

5. Talk of our love for God.

6. Talk of how much God loves us.

7. Talk of God's rules of love - commandments.

8. Talk of God's pain when we hurt ourselves while breaking His commandments.

9. Do you want to hurt God?

10. Imagine that Christ appears in the room -- how do you feel? (Identify the Spirit)

11. You are representatives of Jesus Christ. Challenge to show your love by keeping the commandments and being baptized.

12. Contact them every 24 hours until baptism. (Practice this discussion more than five times before giving it)

THE UNBEATABLE POSITION

1. **THE QUESTIONS**
   a. What do you have to do to be saved?
   b. Do you have to be baptized?
   c. If you have to be baptized, then by whom and how?
   d. Do you need to do any good works?
   e. Are you 'once saved, always saved?'

2. **REPEAT THEIR ANSWERS BACK TO THEM**
   a. Confirm that your understanding of their answers is correct.

3. **DECLARE THAT WE HAVE GREAT NEWS**
   a. By your standards Mormons are going to heaven
   b. All Mormons believe that they have to accept Jesus Christ as their Saviour.
   c. All Mormons are baptized by immersion and by a believer in Jesus Christ.
   d. All Mormons believe in showing their love for the Saviour by keeping His commandments.

4. **OBJECTIONS**
   a. Saved by grace not by works. (So you are saying Mormons are trying to hard?)
   b. Joseph Smith was a false prophet. (If we accept Christ as our Savior, does believing in a 'false prophet' revoke our salvation? Joseph Smith was a false prophet, by your standards Mormons are still going to heaven.)
   c. Mormons don't worship the same Jesus Christ as in the Bible. (John 3:16-18, Acts 4:12 clearly emphasizes that it is the name of Christ by which you are saved. Although we have a different

understanding of the material that God's body is made of, we believe in the teachings, crucifixion and atonement for our sins as taught in the New Testament. Even if we believed Jesus was a polygamist, which we do not, He is still our Saviour by your standards.)

Conclusion: (Pick appropriate response below)

a. So, you should rejoice with us when someone becomes a Mormon, for their salvation is assured by your standards!

b. So, you see, we have all the good things that you have in any other church plus more! There is no disadvantage to being a member of the Church of Jesus Christ of Latter-day Saints. We are saved by your standards!

c. So, what this means, turkey, is that if you are right, and we are wrong, we are still going to Heaven. But if we are right, and you are wrong then you are really missing out!!!

(I'm just joking about choice c. I don't think you convert people with that approach.)

Brothers and sisters, in every mission there has been a Missionary that did not lock their heart and they had to be sent home (or worse). Some Mission Presidents have expressed concern that you will misunderstand the circumstances that led to Sister Marshall and I being married. When I was on my mission I had locked my heart. I did not dwell on getting married even though I was engaged to a girl back home. On the rare occasions that I approached the Lord on the subject, while I was on my mission, I asked the Lord to bless me in this way, that in return for "locking my heart" during my mission, that He would give me a confirmation after my mission as to whom I should marry. I never asked whom I would marry while on my mission. What a blessing it was to make that deal with the Lord. When it was time for me to be married in the Manti Temple the Lord gave me a powerful confirmation that has never diminished that my choice was right. What a blessing! One that was well worth "locking my heart" for. So do not falter! Do not taint the best two years of your life with thoughts and actions of romance that only lessen the gift of service you are giving the Lord (and cause problems for your companion). Make a deal with the Lord that He will give you the mate that is best for you. Not necessarily whom you think is best.

You can make deals with the Lord.

Scott Marshall

The following is an e-mail that I received from President Wagstaff of the Philippines Quezon City mission. President Wagstaff's mission has increased baptisms 300% in seven months! I asked him to share how his mission did it. This is his abridged account. You may e-mail me for the unabridged account. I have underlined key points.

—-Scott Marshall—-

Dear Brother Marshall:

One of the most important factors in our success is our monthly meeting between the Mission President, APs and ZL meeting with the Stake President, Stake Mission President, and others the Stake President invites. <u>During this meeting we have the ZL review with the Stake President each unit in the stake for missionary progress</u>. Such items as: Is there an active WML. How many active Stake Missionaries are there? What training is needed? Who will provide the training? How many member referrals were given? How many baptisms? The ZLs also provide a list of those baptized during the last month as well as a CBC list of each member by unit in the stake. This allows the Stake President to follow up on every new member. We make it a practice to meet with every stake president in our mission every month. <u>If he misses the meeting we call and reschedule</u>. He is not allowed to miss this monthly correlation.

In answer to your question as to how we have been able to increase baptisms I enclose two papers. One is a written description of our view of the baptismal process and the other is a talk by Elder Dyer on the challenging and testifying missionary. In addition to these papers we teach our missionaries to bear their testimony in a special way during the first discussion. After telling the Joseph Smith story, the missionary bears his testimony and then says: <u>Would you like to know how I know that Joseph Smith is a prophet? He then relates a personal experience as to how or why he knows Joseph Smith is a prophet. He makes this experience as humble and as tender and as sacred as possible</u>. This may take up to 15 minutes for some missionaries. <u>Time does not matter</u>. What matters is that the missionary touch the heart of the investigator. When that happens we experience miracles. Investigators are touched by the Holy Ghost, they want to know more about the gospel and <u>they often ask what they can do to learn more. This is when we challenge them to be baptized. This is when we ask them to give us a name of their friend or a family member</u>. This is when we set up to come back and give the rest of the missionary discussions.

MISSIONARY PURPOSE

The primary purpose missionaries are called to serve is TO BAPTIZE. Missionaries often feel that they have been called to gain or build on their own testimony, to help other people learn more about God or to feel better about life, to improve the image of the Church, or to do good for others, etc. While missionaries do accomplish all of the above activities (as well as many personal things) the true purpose of their calling is to baptize. <u>Missionaries must know in their heart that they are on a mission to baptize</u>.

Member Referrals:

The selection of the investigator is essential in this process. It is well known that the best investigator is someone who already knows about or is associated with the Church. More people will be baptized if they come from people pools such as: Part member families, friends or relatives of members. The <u>missionary must have a good association with the Ward Mission Leader</u> who is dedicated to his calling. This association between the missionary and Ward Mission Leader generates more investigators who have an association with the Church. The more member referrals, the more baptisms. Since July, 1998 we have baptized 59 people for every 100 referrals received.

Convert Referrals:

A very important source of investigators is from recently baptized members or from current investigators. <u>Missionaries are asked to invite every investigator who commits to be baptized (either during the first or the second discussion) to provide a referral</u>. We also invite missionaries to be present during the first three discussions of the six new member discussions (these are taught by the stake missionaries). During the first three discussions the missionaries bear testimony and then ask for a referral. <u>Our goal is two referrals per new member</u>.

Marvelous Missionary Award

We also encourage missionaries to work through the Ward and Stake Leadership, the WML and the stake missionaries. The primary role of the members is to provide referrals to the missionaries and to fellowship, to retain, and to nurture those who are baptized. A Marvelous Missionary Award is presented to members who provide a referral who is baptized.

LANGUAGE

The second step in the baptismal process is language. <u>Missionaries must learn the native language of the people</u>. People receive spiritual things much better in their mother tongue. It is very difficult to really be understood in English, especially when it comes to bearing testimony. Conversion only takes place when people "feel" the Spirit. The missionary must be able to help the investigator feel the Spirit of Christ during the teaching process. This happens best in the investigators native tongue.

WHAT TO TEACH

Missionaries teach the six missionary discussions. Often, missionaries will teach a Book of Mormon reading discussion between the first and second discussion. The purpose is to insure that the investigator has fulfilled their commitment to read the Book of Mormon. Missionaries do not proceed with the second discussion until the investigator reads and prays about the Book of Mormon. Investigators must keep these first commitments before other discussions are given. Baptism occurs after the investigators have been given and agree to live the principles included in the six missionary discussions. They must attend at least two (2) sacrament meetings and have lived the Word of Wisdom for at least seven days. They must also pass a baptismal interview.

HOW TO TEACH

We use the missionary guide to obtain the tools to teach. We ask each missionary to obtain the "Master of The Guide Award." This award is given after the missionary memorizes all of the 12 skills and shows that he can apply them in a teaching situation. We know that missionary skills are essential to fully teach the gospel. The missionary guide is essential to good teaching. We also utilize the skills as outlined the presentation entitled: "The Challenging and Testifying Missionary" by Elder Alvin R. Dyer. We subscribe to the idea that we cannot be too aggressive in asking people to be baptized.

MOTIVATION TO ACT

People only change their lives if they feel that they should. No amount of knowledge is sufficient to make people change if they do not feel that they should. We begin this part of the process when missionaries first meet the investigator. When missionaries first meet the new investigator they should make that event memorable. They make the event memorable by doing the following:

<u>Shaking their hand</u>
<u>Looking the investigator in the eye</u>
<u>Saying the investigator's name back to them</u>
<u>Stating their purpose, clearly and with understanding</u>

(The missionary must convey the message that they are here to bring them a great eternal message, one that is really important and one that will benefit the investigator. The investigator is really important and they are going to hear something that will change their life. "I am here to baptize you." "I will not be satisfied until I present to you a message that will change your life." "After you receive it, you will want to be baptized".) The missionary then teaches the first discussion. After teaching the fourth principle, the Joseph Smith principle, the missionary bears their testimony. After this they say: I know that Joseph Smith is a Prophet, and I want to tell you why I know that he is a Prophet. (The missionary then tells the investigator how or why they know that Joseph Smith is a prophet. They make this personal and take as much time as necessary. Time does not matter.) <u>This is the single most important principle that the missionary will teach after testifying that Jesus Christ is The Savior</u>. The investigator must gain a desire to also know that Joseph Smith is a Prophet. <u>IF YOU LEARN NOTHING ELSE, PLEASE LEARN AND USE THIS PRINCIPLE OF TEACHING</u>.

The Special Prayer

The missionary teaches the investigator how to pray and asks them to say a special prayer: Go somewhere private, kneel down and speak vocally, simply ask God if Joseph Smith is His Prophet and if the Book of Mormon is true — then wait for the answer. After teaching about this prayer, the missionary invites the investigator to kneel in prayer and close the first discussion. The investigator is invited to be voice in the closing prayer.

FOLLOW UP

Follow up occurs very early in the teaching process. After the first discussion, the missionary follows up to see if the investigator has read from the Book of Mormon and if he has used the special prayer. After baptism the missionary follows up to see if the investigator has completed the items on the Convert Baptismal Checklist, if they have been confirmed, if they have been given a church calling or been ordained, etc. Follow up is used to help investigators progress through the teaching process and after baptism to help them progress toward the temple endowment and sealing.

Dear Scott:

We received the box of your books yesterday. Thank you so much for sending them. We have received 21 new missionaries and lost 15. As we adjusted for these changes we moved many missionaries and called several to new positions. The mission was really upset with these changes. It settled down by the next week, however, we lost some valuable missionary time. But most importantly we lost the dedication to follow up. Follow up is essential to baptisms. People must really know that we love them enough to check on their progress. Without constant follow up many people will not keep their Word of Wisdom commitments. This is the biggest cause of people not being baptized. Lack of keeping commitments.

We will have new mission records in April, May, and June. First, we had just about 700 member referrals in March and baptisms reflect the previous referral number. Second, we will not make any big changes during these months. In Quezon City we must leave missionaries in areas for at least four months, mostly six months. <u>Our missionaries must learn their areas and they must get the confidence of the members. The longer we leave missionaries in an area the more effective they are</u>. This is a little difficult for new missionaries because they have this desire to "see the mission", to serve in all of the Zones before they go home. Maybe with patience I will come to really understand the mind of the missionary. I pass to you a story that I received on e-mail recently.

Your friend,
President Robert Wagstaff

Do We Really Know What We Have?
As written by Scott Anderson in his journal

We had an unexpected moment in the mission field. We knocked on a door and a lady said something to us we had never heard, "Come in." Now remember, I was a German missionary. This never happened to us; not even the members would say that to us. At this point suddenly this dear lady invited us in. My companion said, "Do you know who we are?" "You want to talk about religion, don't you?" she said. "Yes, we do" explained my companion. "Oh, come in. I've been watching you walk around the neighborhood. I'm so excited to have you here. Please come into my study." We went in and seated ourselves and she sat down behind the desk.

She looked at us with a smile, then pointed to three PhD's hanging over hear head. One in Theology, the study of religion, one in Philosophy, the study of ideas, and one in European History specializing in Christianity. She then kind of rubbed her hands together and said, "Do you see this row of books here?" We looked at a well arranged row of books. She then said, "I wrote them all. I'm the Theology professor at the University of Munich. I've been doing this for 41 years. I love to talk about religion. What would you like to discuss?" My inspired companion said we'd like to talk about the Book of Mormon. She said, "I don't know anything about the Book of Mormon." He said, "I know." Twenty minutes later we walked out of the room. We had handed her a Book of Mormon and this trade off that we had been on was over. I didn't see this lady again for another eight and a half weeks.

It was in a small room filled with people (when I saw her again), as she was standing in the front dressed in white. This Theology professor at the University of Munich was well known throughout Southern Germany. She stood up in front of this small congregation of people and said, "Before I'm baptized I'd like to tell you my feelings. In Amos chapter 8:11 it says there will be a famine of the work of God. I've been in that famine for 76 years. Why do you think I have three PhD's? I've been hungering for truth and have been unable to find it. Then eight and one-half weeks ago, two boys walked into my home. I want you to know these boys are very nice and wonderful young men, but they didn't convert me. They couldn't; they don't know enough." And then she smiled and said, "but since the day they walked in my door I have read the Book of Mormon, the Doctrine and Covenants, the Pearl of Great Price, all of Talmage's great writings, Evidence and Reconciliations by John A. Widtsoe and 22 other volumes of church doctrine." She then said something which I think is a challenge for every one of us here. She said, "I don't think you members know what you have." Then in her quiet, powerful way, she said, "After those years of studying philosophy, I picked up the D&C and read a few little verses that answered some of the greatest questions of Aristotle and Socrates! When I read those verses, I wept for four hours." Then she said again, "I don't think you members know what you have. Don't you understand the world is in a famine? Don't you know we are starving for what you have? I am like a starving person being led to a feast. And over these eight and one-half weeks I have been able to feast in a way I have never known possible."

Her powerful message and her challenging question was then ended with her favorite scripture, "For you don't see the truth can make you free." She said, "these missionaries don't just carry membership in the church in their hands, they carry within their hand the power to make the atonement of Jesus Christ full force in my life. Today I'm going into the water and I'm going to make a covenant with Christ for the first time with proper authority. I've wanted to do this all my life." None of us will forget the day that she was baptized.

When she got finished being baptized, she got back out and before she received the Holy Ghost, she stood and said, "Now

I would like to talk about the Holy Ghost for awhile." She then gave us a wonderful talk about the gift of the Holy Ghost.

(later in Elder Anderson's journal)
Two young missionaries, both relatively new, (one had been out about five months, the other three weeks) accidentally knocked on the door of the seminary in Reagansburg. 125 wonderful men were studying to become priests inside. They didn't realize this was the door they had knocked on because it looked like any other door. They were invited in.

In somewhat of a panic, the man said, "I am sorry we just don't have time right now." The two missionaries were relieved, but then he said, "Would you come back next Tuesday and spend two hours addressing all 125 of us and answer questions about your church?" They agreed that they would, and ran down the road screaming. They made a phone call to the mission president and cried for help. The mission president called us and said, "Do you think that dear lady that you have just brought in to the church would like to come help these two missionaries with this assignment?" I called her to explain what was to happen, and she said, "more than I would like to eat, more than I would like to sleep, more than..." I said, "Fine, you don't have to explain."

We drove her to the seminary and as we went in, she grabbed the two missionaries that had originally been invited, put her arms around them and said, "you are wonderful, young men. Would each of you spend about two minutes bearing your testimony and then sit down and be quiet please?" They were grateful for their assignment. They bore their testimony and then seated themselves. Then she got up and said, "For the next 30 minutes I would like to talk to you about historical apostasy." She knew every date and fact. She had a Ph.D. in this. She talked about everything that had been taken away from the great teachings the Savior had given, mostly organizational, in the first part of her talk. Then the next 45 minutes was doctrinal.

She gave every point of doctrinal changes, when it happened and what had changed. By the time she was done, she looked at them and said, "In 1820 a boy walked into a grove of trees. He had been in a famine just like I have been. He knelt to pray, because he was hungry just like I have been. He saw God the Father and His Son. I know that is hard for you to believe that they could be two separate beings, but I know they are." She shared scriptures that showed that they were and then said, "I would like to talk about historical restoration of truth." She then, point by point, date by date, from the Doctrine and Covenants put back the organizational structure of Christ's church. The last 20 minutes of her talk were absolutely brilliant. She doctrinally put the truth back in place, point by point, principle by principle. When she finished this profound talk, she said, "I have been in a famine as talked about in Amos. You know that because last year I was here teaching you." For the first time, we realized that she was their Theology professor. She continued by saying, "Last year when I was teaching you, I told you that I was still in a famine. I have been led to a feast. I invite you to come." She finished with her testimony and sat down.

What happened next was hard for me to understand. Theses 125 sincere, wonderful men stood and for the next 7 minutes gave a standing ovation. By the time four minutes had gone by I was crying. I remember standing and looking into their eyes and seeing the tears in their eyes too. I wondered why they were applauding after the message she had given. I asked many of them later. They said, "to hear someone so unashamed of the truth, to hear someone teaching with such power, to hear someone who finally has conviction."

The truth is what can set us free... Do we really know what we have?

The next e-mail is from President McKee of the Nevada Las Vegas Mission which is one of the top baptizing missions in the USA. (My underlines)

Box Exercises
MemphisBPC@aol.com

The missionaries are taught if they don't feel a strong spirit in their discussion, to sing. Some missionaries will sing two or three times through a discussion. Periodically in zone conference, we get the box from the Children's Meeting Room pulpit and have each companionship stand on the box and sing to the zone. They actually like it and have fun. It lets them rid themselves of their inhibitions to sing in the homes. Another box exercise is to let each missionary have two-minutes on the box. They pretend they are in England or New York City, preaching the gospel to a crowd. They teach the first and second discussion, using the Principles and Concepts as their outline. They begin with God is our Heavenly Father (First Discussion, First Principle). They can elaborate as long as they want, going through each of that principle's concepts. A missionary timer raises his hand five seconds before the orators two-minutes are up. The timer then stands and remains standing until the orator steps down. The orator stops wherever he is at in the discussion and the next orator will pick-up where he left off. Before the next orator starts preaching, he selects the next "preacher". They can use any method of teaching they want, prose, visual aids, singing, gestures, questions to the crowd, responding to the crowds questions or accusations, and testimony. It's a great confidence builder and the missionaries put a lot into it. We do let the crowd heckle, with some guide lines, like, you can't heckle again until three others have heckled, you must keep the spirit of the exercise. The missionaries are able to see first hand that the greatest influence upon the crowd is when they simply bear their testimony.

The importance of memorizing the Missionary Discussions

Though all missionaries are effective in their teaching (and I really believe that) I found that the missionaries could improve dramatically if they memorized the first and second discussions. We first learn to teach out of the discussion books, using feeling and eye contact.

They cannot pass over the Find Out questions or the designated points to testify. After several months, they actually memorize the first and second discussions (we certify them as teachers, and they re-certify every three months, thereafter). The missionaries universally comment that it was a challenge to memorize the discussions, but it was worth it. They express a greater confidence in their teaching ability and they begin teaching a larger percentage of adults and families. The exercise of memorizing also increases they mental processes and aids them not only in the mission studies and resolving concerns but the exercise and discipline will contribute to their success at school.

The Living Christmas Card

To help the missionaries keep their focus during the holidays and to lift the vision of the members, we proselyte heavily on the holidays. Some feel that we disturb and annoy people if we contact on holidays. I would suggest that the Day of Pentecost was a major Jewish holiday. Peter preached on that great holiday and baptized 3000 the same day!

The fact is, families are gathered at home on holidays. Parents are reflecting on the blessings of their family. We find families to teach and baptize on holidays. These are the best proselytizing days of the year. For consideration, the best proselytizing day of the week is Sunday. Some missionaries use this time to relax and mingle with the members. They really should be out speaking with the neighbors of the members. The missionaries can find more people at home on Sunday than any other day of the week. For Christmas we refined a Living Christmas Card. We begin delivering it on Thanksgiving Day and continue on into January. It provides a teaching pool for several months. It gets us into a lot of doors. The members find is non-threatening to give us the names of their neighbors, friends, co-workers, etc. The card gets members into the excitement of missionary work.

This is how we present the basic card:
We knock on the door. As the door is being opened, the missionaries begin to sing an appropriate Christmas Carol, Away in the Manger, Oh Little Town of Bethlehem, etc. The spirit of the singing catches the attention and spirit of the family. When they finish they say, Tom and Mary Smith, your neighbors John and Judy Bennion asked us to stop by and deliver a Living Christmas Card. May we step in for just a few moments and share with you the story of the birth of the Christ

Child as it is found in Bible? Most people let us in. The visit takes less than 10 minutes. We read Luke 2:1-20, while holding a 5"x7" picture of the Christ Child being held by Mary. <u>Some missionaries have memorized the scripture and take turns reciting it with great feeling and interlacing appropriate carols (powerful presentation). At the conclusion, each bears his witness that Christ is the Redeemer, and they sing another carol, Silent Night, etc</u>. Then they present the family with the picture as a gift and as servants of the Lord leave a blessing on the home. D&C 132:47 'whomsoever ye bless, I will bless'. <u>I teach the missionaries to leave a simple blessing and not one that would threaten the family's beliefs. I suggest they look and listen carefully while they are in the home</u>. They will notice what the family needs. Then bless the family with those needs and the spirit of the Christ Child. Bless the family that love will abound in their home. Bless them that as they live the teaching of the Savior they will have peace. As the missionaries leave, they express their love for the family.

If the missionaries are confident, even the father's are touched and tears come to their eyes. The missionaries will keep a record in their area book as to whom they delivered Living Christmas Cards. <u>I teach the missionaries to leave immediately, so they create with a family the feeling of "Why do you have to leave?"</u>. If the family makes an invitation to stay, the missionaries make a return appoint, within an hour or two if possible. <u>Of course, you can also use this as a tracting door approach, using the same method</u>, you just don't have the advantage of having the person's name.

We use the same format for other holidays; Easter, Mother's Day, Memorial Day, Father's Day, Fourth of July, Labor Day, and Thanksgiving weekend.

Here are some other great ideas:

Virginia Richmond Mission President Allen Feller has dedicated Monday nights as Special Tract For Families Night, using Inspiration Tracting (Chapter 2). What a great way to find families! Kentucky Louisville Mission President Joel Flake attributes his missions great success to: #1 Obedience #2 Work #3 Bold (To be "ripping" Bold!) #4 Skilled in Teaching #5 Sacrifice(Fasting,etc.) #6 Fire! (Great Enthusiasm)

I received the following from the Florida Jacksonville Mission. I am told it came from South America. It is called "The Power Charla" (Spanish for Discussion) It is a correct method for having the Holy Ghost bless your efforts.

The Power Charla

#1 Plan this discussion in detail with companion and any fellowshipping member in advance. Be sure you have a secure quiet location and sufficient time for this discussion.

#2 Fasting will help.

#3 Tell investigator the outline of the discussion, Promise they will feel the Spirit and that God will answer their concern. (Such as "Did Jesus Christ use Joseph Smith as a prophet? Is the Book of Mormon the word of God? etc.)

#4 Sing a spiritual song known to all. Such as "I Believe in Christ" Bring the words—printed.

#5 Express your testimony of Jesus Christ and the most spiritual experience of your life. Ask the Lord to forgive your sins and bless your discussion with the Spirit and an answer to the investigators concern. (Each person at discussion do this individually vocally in turn, Arrange for the investigator to pray last.) Be sure the investigator asks the right question.

#6 Identify the Spirit. This will be a very spiritual moment. Bear strong testimony.

#7 Invite investigator to a specific baptism date. Use a calendar. If this is for a member, commit them to invite someone to family home evening or church.

(This is a discussion I have used with success for years. – Scott)

God's Graph Discussion
(or the Secret of Life Discussion):

You are searching for happiness. Everything everyone does is in search of happiness. For example, you clean a dirty bathroom to gain the happiness of a clean bathroom. I am going to tell you the secret of happiness! Knowing truth about my relationship with God is the secret to happiness, for He loves me and will tell me how to have the greatest happiness in life. Religions claim to have this answer. I have studied the worlds religions for most of my life. I have done so in search of truth about my relationship with God. There nothing anyone learns in life that is more important! (Yet few think deeply about it.) I have come to this conclusion. All religions contain truth, but since they all have different teachings, they must have different degrees of the absolute truth. (that is Gods perception of truth, not ours!) There is no advantage to believing things that are not true!! (Ask the investigator "Is that correct?") Since there is no advantage in learning things that are not true, I want to know which church has the most truth about my relationship with God. This is where happiness can be found. If God were to desire to do so, He could arrange all of the religions of the world on a graph based on how much truth they contain about Him . This graph would start out on the bottom left hand side with the religion that contains the least truth about God and go up to the top right hand side, to the religion with the most truth about God. I wanted to know,"Where was that religion?" I testify in the Name of my Savior Jesus Christ that I have found that church with the most truth about God and His plan for happiness for me! It is the Church of Jesus Christ of Latter Day Saints, and I have lived that happiness for many years. We are here to tell you how you can know this for yourself. (I then would go into what I taught in chapter 7 and/ or chapter 9 with the Spirit)

Callings for new converts

New converts need callings soon after baptism. They should have callings that will not decrease their social relationship in the Ward. It is very important that new converts attend Gospel Essentials and if possible, Relief Society and Priesthood. Certain callings (some in the Primary, for example,) will remove the new converts from associating with their people their own age. If you see this problem, bring it to the attention of the leaders in charge. One of the best callings for a new convert is as a stake missionary.

Speaking to Groups, Organizations, and Media:

Be bold in offering to speak to groups and media. Promise a interesting and positive experience. When speaking to media, offer a list of
prepared questions to the interviewer. Say "Here are some questions
many people would like to know about our Church." You are making
the interviewers job easier,and can direct the flow of the interview in
positive directions. When speaking to groups, plan a full and fast
dynamic presentation. You may show videos. Do not leave time for a
question and answer time. When questions are asked say "We would
like to answer all of your questions, but we must hurry to finish what
we have scheduled to present today. If you will write your name on
the role we are passing around, we will contact you later and answer
all of your questions." Do not speak negatively of any other religion,
people, or anything for that matter. Be positive and smile a lot!

Professional Investigators

Sooner or later every missionary meets the eternal investigator.
Forever learning but never able to be baptized. These people need
special handling - for their sake and for yours. Make very strong
efforts to get them to visit Church. Eliminate all their excuses.
Commit them to set a date by which time they will know that Jesus
Christ used Joseph Smith to restore His Church. This is an important
goal to set for any investigator that will not set a date to be baptized!!
You should spare no effort to bring the Spirit into your discussions.

Also obviously you need to have more than the six standard discussions for slow movers. While I want to emphasize that it is only the
Spirit that converts, gaining an intellectual testimony develops spiritual muscles that fights "anti-forces" and can create more desire to
pray to know Jesus Christ has restored His Church.

President Robison (Michigan, Detroit) recently impressed me with
the great importance of warning of "anti" material just before leaving.
(Especially the first discussion) Do this by clearly identifying the
Holy Ghost that was present. (How did you feel as we taught you?)
Then state "We are authorized servants of Jesus Christ, called by an
Apostle of God and set apart with authority to teach His Gospel. We
are promised that as we teach the truths of His Gospel that the Holy
Ghost will confirm these truths to you. We have found that whenever

110

a person begins to be enlightened with the truth, there is opposition to keep it from happening. This may come from friends, family, ministers, or strangers. You may hear things like: "Don't listen to them! The aren't even Christians" or " They are a cult." When you hear these untrue things, You will feel a darkness very different from the Spirit of Christ you felt as we taught you today. (II Tim. 1:7) When we return we promise that you will feel our Father in Heaven's Spirit even stronger. The things we share with you will bring great joy and happiness into your life!"

The summary of what I have learned about sharing the Gospel is as follows:

1. Inspiration finding is the 1st Core of success.
2. Using every minute to it's highest purpose is the 2nd Core of success. This is my constant focus.
3. Inspiration finding does not limit member missionary work, it enhances it.
   The key to maximizing member missionary work is to time it outside of the "golden finding hours". (In essence 5:30 to 8:30 p.m. Sunday to Thursday). This means to purposefully schedule 5:30 to 8:30 for inspiration finding and try to keep all other work outside of those times. But be determined to get all quality member work done without fail too.
4. Constantly project great enthusiasm to the members and everyone you meet. Tell members exciting short stories constantly!
5. Getting the members to just invite everyone to church with a light, happy, "Why don't you come to visit once? It will be Fun!" is THE best thing to commit the members to do. Then you must follow up on them.
6. Commit the members to use the phase "That's what I love about my Church..." twice a week with non-members!

Resolving The "I've Already Been Baptized" Concern

Loren C. Dunn

"The best way to resolve key concerns is to put them in a position where the Holy Ghost can bear witness to them that our message is true. Your investigators deserve to be on their knees with you.

Baptismal Challenge - Use 2 Nephi 31, you invite to follow the Savior. Always use scriptures.

Objection - You must keep things on their shoulders.

NM:	I've already been baptized.
M:	I see, what you are telling me is that you would be baptized if you haven't been baptized before. Is that right?
NM:	Positive response.
M:	(Call investigator by name and get eye contact), do you really want to know what the Lord wants you to do? (Ask every investigator individually by name.)
NM:	Positive response.
	(Pull out 4 steps of prayer outline.)
M:	Remember when we taught the steps of prayer. (Briefly review the steps of prayer.)
	Do you remember how the Lord answers prayers?
NM:	Response.
M:	(Expound please) Modern revelation tells us that the Lord will tell us in our mind and in our heart that we will feel it is true. If the answer is "no", you will have a radical feeling. If it is "yes" there will be a peace in your mind and heart. (Kneel down, he will quickly follow.)
	I'll put this here.
	(Place the 4 steps of prayer on the ground so the investigator can see them.)
	Now, the question here is if the Lord wants you to be baptized on the 30th. The question is simple; "Heavenly Father, is it your will that I should be baptized into his church on the 30th?
M:	How do you think the Lord would answer your prayer right now?
NM:	Response.
M:	I promise you that the Lord will answer your prayer right now about being baptized. So after you pray, wait until God answers you.
	(Bow your head)
NM:	Investigator prays.
Note:	Do not be the first one to speak after the prayer. The first person to speak loses. In this setting you will find the real concern.
M:	Extend the invitation to baptism.

Objections that may arise:

You Pray

NM:	I'm not good at praying. Why don't you pray?
M:	Thank you. My companion and I have already prayed and we know, it is important for you to know. (Hopefully this will do it.)
NM:	I'd feel uncomfortable praying, you pray.
M:	Okay Mr. Brown, we can all pray. I'll go first, then my companion and then you can go.
Note:	If you have to pray, keep your prayers very simple.

Silent Prayer

NM:	The investigator gives a silent prayer.
M:	I'm sure that was a wonderful prayer. We have come all this way to join our faith with yours. We would love to hear you pray.

Doctrinal Concerns: Don't discuss doctrine, discuss prayer.

Example: "We understand, Bob, but what does the Lord want you to do?"